D1423259

E0000000020285

The Sixth Sense
of Animals

The Sixth Sense of Animals

Maurice Burton

With sixteen pages of photographs by
Jane Burton and 41 illustrations in text

J. M. Dent & Sons Ltd   London

Made in Great Britain
at the
Aldine Press · Letchworth · Herts
for
J. M. DENT & SONS LTD
Aldine House · Bedford Street · London

ISBN 0 460 07869 0

Contents

Plates

Illustrations in the text

Illustrations in text

Introduction

During the last fifty years there has been a most remarkable advance in our knowledge of animal senses. To realize just how great this advance has been one would have had to live through that half-century making a close study of the subject. It can, however, be illustrated by reference to one item alone, the third eye of the New Zealand lizard, tuatara. Fifty years ago virtually all our knowledge of it concerned its structure. Why it was there and what it did were matters for speculation only. To some extent that is still true today, but the methods of investigation have changed vastly. There was talk in the 1920s of a learned savant crawling on his hands and knees over the laboratory floor, following one of these archaic reptiles and holding a lighted candle over its third eye, trying to find out if it was sensitive to light. Today the scientist is more likely to be using an electron microscope or micro-electrodes in pursuit of the same line of research.

Nevertheless stimulating discoveries were even then being made in the laboratories throughout the world and the results were being published in scientific journals. Relatively speaking these were minor discoveries, couched in the esoteric language of the specialist, and awaiting a compiler who would bring them together in a book for the general reader. Such a book was *The Chemical Senses* by R. W. Moncrieff, published in 1944.

One of the next books on animal senses, if not the next, was my own, published in 1961, for a young audience. This was, however, followed by half a dozen others during the next seven years.

As I point out in my next chapter, 1949 can be taken as a watershed in the study of animal senses. It was a year in which we were still marvelling at von Frisch's discoveries about bees and the researches of Griffin and Galambos in America on how bats navigate in the dark. It was also a year in which, unknown to us at the time, we were on the threshold of discovery in the field of bird navigation.

It comes as something of a surprise, therefore, to recall the words of F. Dastoli, written as late as 1968: 'Without the senses of sight, touch, smell, taste or a perception of equilibrium, the question of one's existence is academic. Yet, in spite of the obvious advances in other biological areas—for instance, metabolism, the genetic code and so on—we know very little more about sensors today than we did 143 years ago.' Presumably Dastoli had in mind our fundamental ignorance of what happens at the point of reception. For example, an odour reaches the cells in the smell membrane in our nostrils and we have a good idea how this happens. A message passes from the smell membrane through nerves to the brain. The impulses constituting the message have been tracked along the nerves and measured, the part of the brain receiving the message has been located and studied. What we still do not know is how the molecules of odour in the air are transducted into the impulses passing along the nerves.

Apart from our profound ignorance on this point there has been an overwhelming accumulation of information in the last twenty to thirty years, far too much to bring conveniently into one book. This is why the half-dozen authors of the books on animal senses has each chosen a different approach and has selected different aspects of the subject. This present volume must, I feel sure, differ markedly from the others in many respects, although obviously similar in fundamentals.

For any virtue this present book may possess I am indebted to all those authors whose works I have read, whether these be articles in scientific journals or books written for the non-specialist reader. I have carried out no experiments, either outdoors or in the laboratory, and am filled with admiration for the skill and patience of those who have. My approach has been that of observing the living animal, seeing what it does and relying on what I read to help interpret its behaviour. This has been a never-ending source of interest and I can only hope that I have conveyed something of this in the pages that follow.

Chapter 1

Threshold of discovery

Jim Phelan, author, who had spent fourteen years in prison, wrote: 'The tyro in jail has not only to learn a new language and become adept in minor trickeries. He has to develop new senses, become animal-keen in a thousand ways not known to civilization. Long before the end of my second year I could tell one warder from another, in the dark and at a distance, by his breathing, by his scent, even by the tiny crackings of his joints. Presently I could smell a cigarette in another man's pocket six feet away, hear a lip-still mutter in church even while a trained warder missed every sound. From the way an official clears his throat a long-term prisoner will know whether that man is likely to report him for smoking half an hour later—a long-sentence convict is not a person, he is an alert, efficient and predatory animal.'

Phelan wrote these words more than twenty years ago, at a time when all but a minority of zoologists were comfortably complacent that while we might have a deficient sense of smell, as compared with a dog, for example, our other senses, and especially our vision, compared favourably with those of most animals. That year, 1949, could almost be taken as a frontier between the old knowledge and the new, in the field of animal senses. It was a year in which the full implication of the discovery about bats' use of echo-location was about to be felt, as well as von Frisch's remarkable discoveries about bees' use of the sun's position in the sky. It was also the year that preceded discoveries about birds' use of celestial navigation that was to have such a profound effect on the whole world of natural history.

Events in the years 1939–46 had caused a slowing down in the more academic scientific research, but under pressure of military necessity, inventions had been made and perfected that were later to be used in biological investigation, in the laboratory and in field studies. Radar is an outstanding example, and hardly less important was the German invention of the infra-red telescope which could be used in studying the behaviour of nocturnal animals. The use of these and the electron microscope, as well as the use of micro-electrodes, gathered force in the early 1950s.

The statement that there are five senses, touch, taste, smell, sight and hearing, was sufficient until about the year 1940. There was, however, always the lurking suspicion that there might be a sixth sense, although nobody had any clear ideas about what this might be. This sixth sense was always vague and indefinable and came rather to express a means of communication that could not be linked with the five primary senses. Today it is not just a question of whether or not there is a sixth sense, but of just exactly how many additional senses there are.

Perhaps we can start most profitably by assessing just how mani-fold—and, indeed, remarkable—are the advances made in the field of animal senses during the last twenty to thirty years. Before that time our explanations of how the senses worked was about as elementary as our cataloguing of the senses themselves. For example, it used to be said, and for that matter still is said, that the eye works like a camera. So far as basic principles are concerned this is still true, yet there are important qualifications to be made. In a camera, the light from the object being photographed passes through a lens and falls on a sensitized film. There it is recorded permanently. In the eye, light passes through a lens and falls on a sensitive layer, the retina, which makes no permanent record. Instead the energy represented by the light waves passes through the optic nerve to the brain where some-thing of the nature of a permanent record is made, which can be examined (that is, recalled) with the aid of memory. There will, however, be a considerable difference between the image of the object recalled by even the best memory and the image preserved on photographic film, which is why eye-witness testimony must be used with extreme caution.

On their way from the outside world to the retina the light waves are modified by accessory structures such as the pupil of the eye and the lens. Some energy is filtered, and from the moment the light waves reach the eye information is being selected from the bewilder-ing array that is bombarding it. Thus the pupil expands or contracts automatically according to the amount of light falling on the eye. In bright light it contracts so that the amount of light entering is cut down, and the eye is not blinded. The cornea and lens, in turn, focus light on the receptor cells of the retina, so that the information they pass on is more detailed.

The receptor cells in the retina are not sensitive only to one par-ticular energy form, such as light. It is, in fact, possible to 'fool' the brain by pressing the eyes with the fingers. The pressure stimulates the receptor cells in the retina and the brain interprets this as light. That is why we see brilliant flashes when we are struck a blow on the eye.

The difference, therefore, between the eye and the camera is that in the first there has been modification, filtering and decoding, and other things besides, instead of a straightforward record of the scene in front of it, as in a camera.

A traditional remark is 'seeing is believing'. In the light of what has been said even that, seemingly so firmly beyond dispute, must now be taken cautiously. Those who make a specialist study of the conscious control of the body maintain emphatically that we cannot trust our senses, a view more closely in accord with modern scientific advances. When we are dealing with animal senses we have to proceed even more cautiously. One of the revolutions of the past half-century is that whereas it used to be assumed that the only world was the one bounded by the limits of our senses, we now realize that there are sensory worlds outside our own, some of them almost unbelievable. There are sights, sounds and smells beyond our ability to perceive, although we know they exist, and these frontiers are continually being pushed further back. It has long been known that a dog's ability to pick up odours is far keener than our own, that cats can see in the dark, that some owls can hear the faint rustlings of mice in leaf litter, that a bee can find its way home if taken a mile from the hive and released, but the full extent of this greater sensitivity of the senses could not be appreciated until appropriate techniques had been devised for probing and testing them. In a similar way, animal sensory abilities could not be fully interpreted or explored until appropriate techniques, often devised for entirely different purposes, had been elaborated.

The long-standing mystery of how bats find their way about in the dark was finally solved in the years around 1940. The realization that they were using ultrasonics was a breakthrough, and in the intervening years it has resulted in the discovery that one animal after another is using sounds we cannot hear for communicating with its fellows, searching for food, escaping from enemies or for finding its way.

At times new discoveries come tumbling over one another and there is the temptation to leap ahead. This sometimes results in a whole generation of scientists being taken along a wrong track. The concept of conditioned reflexes is typical, and this is an appropriate point to consider this important subject.

A conditioned reflex is a simple form of learning, and experiments

3

using the conditioned reflex have been widely employed for finding out just how sensitive a sense organ may be. The technique was made famous by Pavlov's experiments on dogs. He was studying the mechanism controlling the secretion of digestive juices, and the discovery of the conditioned reflex came as a side issue. When meat is placed in its mouth a dog automatically salivates. The saliva lubricates the food, making it easier to swallow. This is a reflex action, over which the dog has no control. Pavlov noticed that a dog started to salivate before the food was put into its mouth or even before it could see or smell it, when it saw that its attendants were getting ready to feed it. He took this a step further, ringing a bell just before giving the dog food until it was so conditioned that it salivated when the bell was rung, even if it was given no food.

Pavlov had established the principle that a simple reflex (e.g. salivation at the sight of food) can be triggered by a completely different stimulus (e.g. a bell ringing) merely because of its association with it and without any end result.

Unwittingly Pavlov had put a useful tool into the hands of those studying animal senses. If a dog is trained to associate a whistle with food it is possible to find out the upper limit of a dog's hearing by using a Galton whistle—the so-called silent whistle—adjusting it for higher and higher notes until the dog fails to salivate when the whistle is blown.

The method was also used for assessing the colour vision of bees. Karl von Frisch devised a long series of experiments in which bees were conditioned to associate a particular colour with the presence of food. He arranged a number of squares of paper of the same size and shape but of different colours near a bee-hive. He put a watch-glass with sugar solution in it on one of the colours and put empty watch-glasses on the others. The sugar solution was odourless and colourless. After repeating this until the bees had learned to go to this particular square von Frisch omitted the sugar solution, yet the bees still went to the same colour. By extending the experiments he established that bees cannot distinguish between red, black and dark grey, between orange-yellow and orange-red or between blue and violet. So a bee cannot see colours as well as we can.

Von Frisch was cautious. It could have been that it was brightness that attracted the bees. He carried out a series of experiments, using shades of grey, that eliminated this possibility. Lubbock years ago had found that ants are sensitive to ultra-violet rays. Von Frisch covered his squares of coloured paper with a sheet of glass to eliminate, or at least minimize, the amount of ultra-violet being transmitted. In the end he could plot the visible spectrum for a honey bee and show it to be different from that for man.

Many experiments of this kind were carried out, but they were all very time-consuming. Thus, in trying to find the highest note a dog can hear, dogs of various breeds had to be trained and each one had to be tested several times. Moreover it was not certain that the correct deductions were being made, as, for example, when the same tests were carried out on guinea-pigs. There the conclusion was reached that guinea-pigs had a poor sense of hearing until it was realized that their reaction to sound was to keep still.

This was not the only time the investigators have been misled. Another classic example is that of the ampullae of Lorenzini. These are pits in the skin of the heads of skates and rays, the flat fishes related to sharks. When these are subject to slight pressure the fish reacts, as it does when heat is applied to the ampullae. In a dictionary of biological terms published as recently as 1963 the ampullae of Lorenzini are defined as 'temperature receptors'. Since then it has been found that the ampullae are highly sensitive to electric currents, the fish's reaction to these being far greater than to pressure or temperature. For example, the ampullae are capable of detecting electrical activity in the muscles of another fish, even one lying still on the sea bed. The ampullae are therefore highly sensitive detectors of prey.

Fortunately there are today many more ways of studying a particular sense-organ. About forty years ago, for example, the technique of nerve tapping began. This is like telephone tapping on a much smaller scale. An electrode is inserted into the body of an animal, which is equivalent to earthing it, and another is connected to a nerve fibre. The electric currents passing along the nerve can be registered and amplified in a loudspeaker so that each impulse is heard as a click, or it can be seen as a trace on an oscilloscope. With the electrodes in position a wide range of stimuli can be applied to a particular sense-organ in a relatively short space of time, from which one can learn which stimuli produce the greatest reaction.

Messages passing along a nerve are, however, from the sense-organ as a whole because each nerve is made up of hundreds of fibres, each carrying its own message. So it was necessary to use micro-electrodes which could be implanted in single fibres. Even more delicate micro-electrodes were devised, that detect even more minute electric charges in the various parts of the cell, such as the charge spreading across the membrane of a receptor cell that triggers the nerve impulse.

Concurrent with the development of the micro-electrodes came the invention of the electron microscope. Prior to this, minute structures in animal tissue could only be studied with the ordinary light microscope, which gives a practical magnification of not more than a thousand times. In an electron microscope these sections of tissue are bombarded with a stream of electrons instead of light waves, and magnifications of 45,000 times are possible.

The more refined the techniques the narrower is the investigator's field of vision, not only in a literal sense but in the sense that he is apt to forget that the tiny structure he is examining is only a minute part of the whole animal. So there is a divorce between what we know of the workings of the sense-organs and the use the animal makes of these organs in its everyday life. The gulf is not easy to bridge. It seldom, if ever, happens that a scientist skilled in the use of the electron microscope or micro-electrodes has more than a passing knowledge of animal behaviour, while the ethologist, the student of animal behaviour, is aware of the finer laboratory researches to a limited degree only. We may go even further and say that the ethologist often derives his information from laboratory experiments or observation of animals in captivity, so that he may not be fully equipped to equate his results with what can be observed of the animal living free in the wild.

It may be that in fifty years' time, assuming that discoveries continue at their present rate, a more closely integrated story can be told. At present we can only examine the primary senses one by one, study how these contribute to the new developments in the wider fields of sonar, electrogenic organs and celestial navigation, and wonder what other extraordinary revelations may be made in the years to come.

Chapter 2

The importance of touch

In an evolutionary sense, we can parody the Book of Genesis and say: 'In the beginning there was touch.' It is about as reasonable a statement as any in describing how sense-organs started, although it can also be argued that the sense of smell may have come first. According to the current view, all life, plant or animal, has evolved from an almost structureless, minute unit of protoplasm, able to do little more than move about, feed itself and reproduce. It must, however, have been able to feel its way, and by this argument touch must be the earliest of the senses, and that is why we deal with it first.

In dealing with the senses one is compelled to take them one by one, and it becomes solely a matter of personal choice which should come first. Admittedly my choice of touch is intuitive and therefore difficult to justify by logical argument. There are two ways of approaching this. The first is to try to envisage the way of life of the first animals ever to appear on this planet. If our current views are anywhere near to being correct, that must have been three thousand million years ago or more, and the first animals would have been little better than the simplest organisms we can envisage—something of the order of bacteria—but capable of movement. In trying to project our minds back into such a distant past we are groping even more than in trying to probe the innermost secrets of how the senses of present-day animals work. For if we have to grope, and the pages that follow will show how much we do, when dealing with animals we can handle, touch and observe, how much more uncertain we are in trying to reach a decision on the first animals which can never be more than figments of our imagination.

The second line of approach is to seek comparisons with animals living today. For example, at what point in the development of an animal, from the first division of the fertilized egg, do the various senses appear, and which of these play the first role in the perceptions of the developing individual? We can, by examining embryos under the microscope, watch the eyes appear, the ears take shape, the

7

nostrils form, even the tongue unfurl. But touch is such a generalized sense that it is difficult to locate it at such an early stage.

We turn therefore to what happens as the new individual enters the world beyond the egg membranes or the womb, as the case may be. One of the first examples to come to mind is the newly born kangaroo, because it reaches the outside world while still in the early stages of development. Its eyes are not yet open. Its ears, so far as we can tell, are not yet functioning as organs of hearing. It may have, and almost certainly has, the beginnings of a sense of smell, possibly also of taste, although this is more doubtful. Its first action must be to crawl through its mother's fur from the exit of her birth-canal to the opening of her pouch in which it will spend the next few months holding one of her teats in its mouth and doing little more than imbibing milk and growing. Unlike the adult kangaroo with which we are familiar, the newly born kangaroo has small hind legs and long forelegs. It is with the latter that it pulls itself through the fur—using a sense of touch?

But why does it go upwards, which is the only way it can reach the pouch of the mother who is squatting on her haunches while the birth is taking place? Presumably it is moving against gravity, which means it has an appropriate sense to register this, and this almost certainly will be in the inner ear.

One of the important lessons to be learned from the birth of a kangaroo, the details of which were revealed firmly only a few years ago, is how effective the senses can be with a minimum of nervous tissue, for the brain of the newly born kangaroo is still in the very early stages of its development.

Perhaps we can try to assess the relative importance of the sense of touch along another avenue of inquiry. A person can lose the sense of sight and still lead a fairly full life. The loss of the sense of hearing is equally unpleasant but less of a handicap. Many people have lost their sense of smell, possibly their sense of taste. Helen Keller was born blind, deaf and dumb, yet through her sense of touch, almost miraculously, led a very full life.

If no other argument prevails, perhaps we can say that the sense of touch is the least destructible of the primary senses because it is sited all over the body. Eyes can fail, ears cease functioning, taste and smell degenerate, but without the total destruction of the body touch still lingers on.

Finally, touch is fundamental to procreation, the continuance of life, if only in the sense of contact—from the coming together of conjugants of the single-celled animals, in the verification for a spermatozoon that it has reached an ovum to fertilize it, right up through the animal kingdom to the sophisticated courtship and mating in the upper levels of animal life.

In its simplest form, the sense of touch is no more than a general sensitivity in the cells of the skin. More specialized organs of touch are of two kinds, simple twig-like nerve endings in the skin and corpuscles in which the nerve ends in a speck of jelly enclosed in concentric layers of supporting cells. The corpuscles lie close beneath the surface of the skin and in ourselves are most numerous on the finger-tips, the palms of the hands and the soles of the feet, the backs of the hands and the tip of the tongue.

The sensitivity of human skin can be tested with two pins or two stiff bristles pressed against the skin of a blindfolded person to see how close together they must be brought before that person feels one pinprick. On the back of the hand the two points can be distinguished when 32 mm apart, on the palm 11 mm apart and on the finger-tip only 2 mm apart. On the tip of the tongue, the most sensitive part of the body, the distance is 1 mm, which is why an ulcer or a gap between the teeth, touched by the tip of the tongue, feels so large.

Touch must be a particularly important sense to many animals, especially those in the lower reaches of the animal scale. One of the most lowly of the multi-celled animals are the sponges. They lack any form of brain or nerve, they have no eyes or organs of hearing. They live rooted to the spot, drawing their food towards them. Whether they have any sense of smell or taste nobody can tell. Most of them appear to have no feeling whatever and yet there are some that seem to shrink when touched, and it may be we shall eventually find that their paramount sense is that of touch.

Any animal, such as a sponge, which remains fixed to one spot has less need of touch than animals moving about, since the primary function of touch is that of registering contacts and collisions. There are, however, special developments of it that are used as senses for recognizing lengths and shapes, as in spiders and bees.

The sense of touch can also be highly developed in humans. Skilled bakers can detect differences in the water content of otherwise similar doughs of as little as 2 per cent by differences in their stickiness. Cloth feelers in the textile trade compare the qualities of cloth by touch. Moreover they can still do this with their finger-tips coated with a layer of collodion, which forms an artificial skin over the finger-tips. Many can judge a cloth by tapping it with a stick which acts as an extension to the sense-organs and this helps us understand how a crab, with its hard outer skeleton, can have a well-developed sense of touch. From the example of the cloth feelers, also, we gain an idea of how quickly the sense works. Merely touching the cloth with a stick for one three-hundredth of a second enables them to test its quality.

We can compare the cloth feeler's stick with hairs in our skin, which have nerve-endings associated with their roots and with the walls of the pit from which the hair springs. When pressure is exerted on a hair it gives the sensation of touch without actual contact with the skin.

Touch, however, has two primary disadvantages. First, it requires 100 million to 10,000 million times as much energy to produce a sensation as does hearing or vision. These seemingly exaggerated figures serve to stress the extremely minute units of energy required to stimulate other sense-organs: one quantum of light registers on a visual sense cell, vibrations of subatomic proportions excite the ear, the smell can depend on a single molecule. Later, when we have to deal with electric organs, we shall have to deal in micromicroampères, each of which is one billionth of an ampère.

Secondly, there is the question of fatigue. When we touch something lightly the finger-tip quickly becomes fatigued and its touch organs less sensitive, but to compensate for this there is a reflex action. The tip of the next finger becomes more sensitive as the other one tires. This may or may not account for a lobster having 50,000 to 100,000 tactile bristles, organs of touch, scattered over its big claws and legs alone.

The statistics given in this last paragraph may be impressive, yet they advance our study of the subject but little. Equally, one may contemplate the anatomy of the organs of touch to little profit. What is more satisfying is to see how deeply the sense of touch can affect the lives of individual animals from early infancy.

A most striking experiment was carried out some years ago with baby rats. A third of the babies chosen were kept in one cage, adequately fed and cared for so far as warmth and general hygiene were concerned, but they were never handled. An equal number were treated similarly, but were given mild electric shocks for a set number of minutes each day. The third group were under identical conditions, but were gently handled as often and for as long as the second group were given their electric shocks.

As the rats grew up those that were left alone, that is, not handled or shocked, were timid, cowered in corners, urinated frequently and were unable to endure extremes of temperature or other physical hardships. When subjected to the standard laboratory tests for problem solving, that is the usual 'intelligence' tests, they showed themselves to be markedly subnormal.

The second group, surprisingly, showed no ill effects from the repeated shocks. They were, in fact, more or less normal rats, although they did not compare with the third group, which had been handled. These were markedly more friendly than those in the other two groups, more intelligent, more healthy and more able to stand up to rigorous treatment. They were more resistant to heat and cold, to starvation and to fatigue.

There is a parallel here with the well-known experiments by Harry F. Harlow of the University of Wisconsin with artificial mothers for baby monkeys. At the age of two days each baby was given a mechanical 'parent' of the same size as its mother fitted with a teat supplying warm milk. One parent was no more than a wire cage. Another was made of wood covered in foam rubber with a layer of towelling over that. Both parents had movable heads with reflectors for eyes, and both were slanted backwards so that the baby could position itself comfortably on the 'mother' when feeding.

Both babies readily went to the artificial mother to suckle, but the one with the wire cage for its mother never went to it when disturbed or frightened, but, like the baby rats that were never handled, tended to cower in a corner and hide its eyes under its arms, even scream, when circumstances were not normal or when it was confronted with some terrifying object. The second baby was far more contented, would spend much time on its cloth-covered parent, hugging it, nestling into it, turning the mother's head round and sitting on its shoulders. When presented with the same terrifying object as the other baby it would, after brief hesitation, go over and examine it, not run away from it or be terrified by it. The soft touch of the towelling mother somehow gave the baby monkey a sense of comfort and security.

This is one aspect only of the workings of the sense of touch, but it is an aspect which, on the face of it, we would expect to be exclusive to the higher animals. The relations between hermit crabs and sea anemones make this slightly doubtful.

Hermit crabs have a soft, twisted abdomen and for greater protection they use the empty shell of a sea snail in which to live. Some hermit crabs carry a sea anemone on this shell, a fact that is well known because the story has been told so often in books on natural history. In its usual form the story goes that by this partnership the anemone protects the hermit crab from its enemies and is rewarded by sharing the food the hermit crab catches and tears to pieces. There is little evidence for this, in fact the partnership is much more complicated, but the more interesting feature is in the way it comes about.

In European seas there are three kinds of hermit crab that carry the sea anemone about, and the way the anemone gets onto the hermit crab's shell differs in each case. One crab lifts the anemone onto its shell, the second strokes the anemone with its claws to persuade it to come onto the shell and the third does nothing except station itself near the anemone, which climbs on of its own accord.

All three involve the sense of touch, and in the second method, in which the anemone is being stroked by the hermit crab, touch is being used to trigger off a particular behaviour pattern, that of the anemone climbing onto the shell.

The most interesting of all is the third method. In this the anemone, without any obvious inducement from the hermit crab, explores the shell it occupies with its tentacles, some of which adhere to the shell by means of certain of their stinging cells, which are sticky. As more and more of the tentacles adhere to the shell the mouth is more closely drawn to its surface until it touches it. Then the anemone contracts its muscles, pulling the mouth up, so creating a vacuum between the mouth and the shell. Temporarily the mouth becomes a sucker. Once it has done this the anemone cannot be dislodged by the hermit crab. After a few minutes it brings its foot over, becomes firmly attached and raises its body to the normal position. The whole operation seems to be guided solely by the sense of touch.

The hermit crab, as it grows too large for the shell it is occupying, must find a new and bigger shell to live in. It searches around, testing each empty shell it encounters with its claws. It has eyes, but from the way it works it seems more likely that touch plays the main part in deciding whether the new shell is of the right size. The hermit crab runs its claws over it and inside it, then, as if satisfied, it grips the rim of the new shell with its claws and with one quick flip transfers its soft abdomen from the old home to the new.

If there is an anemone on the hermit crab's shell when the transfer takes place, it creeps down from the old shell, explores the new one with its tentacles and goes through the actions we have described to fasten itself onto the new shell.

It may be that in selecting a larger shell the hermit crab uses its claws as callipers to gauge the size. There is no evidence to prove this or to disprove it. But if the hermit crab is not using this as a method there are other animals that do so.

The comb of the honeybee is made up of hexagonal cells. The bees are able to feel the size of the cell as they are building it. This is evident from the uniform pattern of the comb. Moreover some cells are larger. These are reserved for the production of drones (the males). When the queen comes to lay her eggs she must be able to tell the smaller worker cells from the larger drone cells, and this she does by measuring them with bristles on either side of her abdomen.

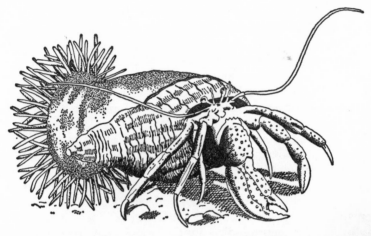

Hermit crab in its house, an empty whelk shell, with its mess-mate, a commensal sea anemone. Practically the only means of communication between these two animals, which live in such close association, is through the sense of touch.

The evidence for the use of touch in judging sizes is more clear cut in the researches made by D. Merrill on why caddis worms stop building. These larvae of caddis flies live in fresh waters. They have long bodies protected by a tube of silk threads strengthened by pieces of stick or leaf, tiny pebbles, even small shells of water snails. The tube reaches from the insect's head to its tail, just long enough for it to cling by hooks on its rear end while pushing its front part out to drag the tubular case around and to feed.

Merrill decided that the caddis worm used sensory bristles on the hind end of the abdomen as measuring instruments, so he took one of the larvae and cut off these bristles. When put back into the water the larva started to build a new case, and went on building until the case was three times as long as it should be—then gave up from sheer exhaustion. Without its bristles the larva had no means of telling that it had built a large enough case.

H. Peters tried, by painstaking research, photographing spiders on their webs and deducing from mathematical considerations, to find out how it came about that the webs were built in such a regular design. He came to the conclusion that spiders use their legs to measure the angles in the web. His conclusions were tentative, but they seem not unreasonable. Although his calculations and his evidence are both too long and too complicated to be briefly summarized, it is possible to believe in them if only because of what can be seen in animals of similar capacity.

A female hunting wasp digs a vertical shaft in sandy ground in which to lay an egg. She then flies off to intercept a bee. She knocks it to the ground and paralyses it with a quick thrust of her sting, then carries it off to the shaft, drags it down, lays an egg on it and closes the entrance to the shaft. The larva hatching from the egg finds a living but immobile bee—a supply of fresh meat—on which to feed.

This story, or others like it, has been told about hunting wasps again and again, always giving the impression that the wasp has only to find the soft joint in the bee's armour into which it can insert its sting. W. Rathmayer, in 1962, found it was less simple than this. Except for one tiny spot on the bee's underside just behind where the first pair of legs join the body, a bee's cuticle is too tough for the wasp's sting to penetrate. The hunting wasp must quickly find this one vulnerable spot and insert its sting without delay, or it will itself be stung by the bee. To help it in this it has a highly specialized organ of touch with which it finds the exact spot.

In other words, this is no haphazard stabbing by the hunting wasp but a skilled surgical operation. The animal world, especially the insect world, is probably teeming with similar examples of skill awaiting discovery by researchers with the perspicacity of Dr Rathmayer. There are probably as many surprises yet to come concerning the use of whiskers, or vibrissae as they are better called.

A mole lives an unusual life, almost in perpetual darkness, and although it has eyes these are very small. They serve possibly to distinguish night from day, and little more besides this. A mole is said to have an acute sense of smell, yet this is difficult to prove. It has no ear flaps, or pinnae, as they should properly be called, but the general opinion is that its hearing is acute. If so, this is remarkable, because as a rule those animals that have acute hearing also have large pinnae. Even Shakespeare, writing at a time when knowledge of animals was as crude as it could be, wrote: 'Tread softly, that the blind mole may not hear a foot fall.' It could be that the mole's sensitivity is due to acute hearing or to an ability to pick up vibrations in the ground.

At all events, up until twenty years ago or even more recently, all that was said as a rule by authors writing on moles was that they had no eyesight worth mentioning, acute hearing and smell, and a sensitivity to vibrations. They did not even specify whether it was vibrations reaching the mole through the earth, from a footfall, for example, or through the air, or both.

Even in those days there were some of us who suspected, merely by watching a mole in its daily behaviour, that it must have sense-organs of touch of an unusual kind, and we looked at the long bristles that decorate its head, and the snout more particularly, that could be either touch receptors or vibration receptors, or both. For one thing, when we examine the skin of the head under a high-power microscope, we find that at the base of each bristle where it is implanted in the skin there is a knot of fine nerves surrounded by a plexus of minute blood-vessels. This alone suggested a high sensitivity.

Research since then has revealed an unusual equipment of organs of touch. Some of these may be so delicate as to serve as 'touch at a distance', that is, detecting minute vibrations in the soil which may come from other animals, even as small as worms, moving some distance away. Little is known about this sensitivity, but a mole's skin has more touch organs than that of any other mammal. There are hundreds of tiny pimples (papillae), known as Eimer's organs, on the tip of the snout. Each consists of a bunch of nerve-endings and several sensitive cells, and deeper in the skin beneath it are blood sinuses. When the mole is probing with its snout blood rushes into these sinuses and the tip of the snout becomes larger and swollen and very red. Each of the Eimer's organs has a tiny, sensitive hair embedded in it. There are sensitive hairs also on the tail, used as organs of touch when a mole is moving backwards through its tunnels, which it can do easily as the fur has no set. That is, which-ever way it is stroked the fur does not look untidy.

A mole also has sensitive organs on its body, especially on the belly, known as Pinkus' plates. They were first discovered by F. Pinkus, in the early years of this century, in human beings. So far they have been found only in man, the cat and the mole. Pinkus' plates are similar to Eimer's organs, but how they function and what purpose they serve in the mole are at present unknown, except that they are almost certainly organs of touch. The fact that there are so many of them suggests that they are important, yet it is difficult even to guess how sense-organs hidden under the fur can operate.

The importance of touch

So far as the mole's bristles are concerned we are still very much in the dark, but we can guess at their function from the very few pieces of solid information we have from other species. One of the most startling is from the desert jerboa, a rodent with long hind legs, a long tail and very long whiskers. It spends the day in its burrow and comes out at night to leap like a kangaroo over the desert sands in search of seeds. Among the bristles on its head are two that are nearly as long as its body. These hang straight down and are always in touch with the ground, except when the jerboa jumps high. Even then, they are

Stylized picture of a desert jerboa *Jaculus jaculus* in the act of leaping, its short forelegs drawn up into its fur. Wholly nocturnal, with the large eyes of a night forager, the jerboa depends on touch to a high degree. The long whiskers, we are told, keep contact with the ground all the time it is bounding along.

at most temporarily off the ground and are probably the first part of it to touch the ground when the rodent lands. They keep the rodent apprised of the configuration of the ground's surface and of any obstacle in its path.

The tail also is hanging down and in touch with the ground, but its main function is to press quickly onto the ground and steer the rodent to right or left, even in mid-jump, on receipt of a signal through the brain, from the two long bristles in front. But it is also acting as an organ of touch.

Nearer home, the cat's whiskers have long attracted notice even from non-zoologists, and there is a general acceptance that the whiskers are organs of touch helping the cat to feel its way in the dark. It has even been claimed that a cat may sometimes detect the presence of a crouching mouse with its whiskers. The general function must be, however, as feelers, in much the same way as a man walking along an unlighted corridor at night, if he is wise, holds his hands in front with fingers extended, waving them about, to feel for possible obstacles.

Because these whiskers are used mainly at night it is difficult for us to make a close study of how they work. It is significant, however, that if you cradle a cat on your hands and swing it to and fro in the air the whiskers move in conjunction. When the cat is at rest its whiskers lie backwards, more or less along the side of the head. As the cat is swung forwards its whiskers also swing forwards, reaching well in front of the face. Some dogs have longer whiskers than others, and one can cradle a smallish dog in one's arms and swing it to and fro with the same result as with the cat. An otter too brings its whiskers automatically into play as soon as it starts to move.

When a seal pushes its head above water its whiskers lie back along the side of its face. The moment it submerges its head, and the whiskers are below the surface, they are swung forward. These actions are so automatic that there can be little question that the whiskers are used under water, either to pick up vibrations or as organs of touch, and probably both.

A walrus is in effect a large seal with long tusks. It feeds by diving, often into deep water, to gather clams with its mouth. Around the mouth is a battery of hundreds of whiskers sprouting from the upper lip. These are long and so stout they could almost be used for knitting needles if they were straight instead of being curved. Nobody has studied closely how a walrus's whiskers work because walruses live in arctic seas and feed in deep, murky waters—not the best conditions for close scientific research. We may guess, however, that in its search for clams the walrus uses the whiskers as the cloth feeler can use a stick to feel cloth.

Chapter 3

Keeping the right way up

Crustaceans are animals with a tough coat which is so inelastic that in order to grow in size they must shed this coat periodically. Every few weeks or months, according to the size of the animal, the coat splits down the back and the crustacean, whether it be lobster, prawn, crab or woodlouse, pulls itself out leaving behind its old coat. Its body is now soft and is covered by a new coat which must harden. During this vulnerable period the crustacean must hide. When the coat has hardened the crustacean comes out of hiding and resumes a normal life. For some prawns, however, there is still one more thing remaining to be done.

If we could watch one of these prawns closely at such a time we would see it pick up sand grains with its claws and drop a few into each of two holes near where its antennae spring from the body.

One of the more difficult movements carried out by a ballet dancer is the pirouette. In this, the dancer whirls rapidly round and round on her points, so fast that the details of her body are blurred. But we can still see her face because this does not keep time with the body. The dancer has to learn not to revolve the head continuously in time with the body but by quick turns. In this way the head is not spinning but turning quickly with brief pauses between each turn. Without this trick the organs of balance in the head would be thrown into confusion, and when the pirouette was finished the dancer would be dizzy and unable to continue.

Improbable as it may seem, the prawn and the ballet dancer are both doing much the same thing: taking steps to ensure that they stay the right way up.

As soon as the first animals started to move about, they needed some means of keeping themselves in an orderly state in relation to their environment as well as to other organisms. They needed, in other words, to keep themselves the right way up and to keep themselves going in the right direction. So they would have had to have organs of balance and orientation, no matter how simple. Only two physical influences in their world, gravity and light, were reasonably stable. Gravity is the more unchanging and has been more commonly used, but light also played a part. We ourselves have organs of balance in our ears and we also use our eyes to keep upright, and we use both of these also to walk straight.

How do we retain our balance when standing or moving around, or for that matter when we are sitting? One need only try standing still for a moment to realize that we are kept upright by continuous minor adjustment of muscles. And the key to the control is in our inner ear, in two cavities, or sacs, known as the sacculus and utriculus. They are filled with fluid and each has a patch of fine hair-like sensory cells, the macula. Microscopic calcareous, or chalky, granules rest on these, and as long as our position is vertical the granules, under the pull of gravity, will press vertically down on the maculae. As our body moves out of the vertical the hairs are tipped to one side and the granules bend them over, so stimulating the nerves leading from them. Messages are carried to the cerebellum, a thickened part of the hind-brain, and in conjunction with messages from other position receptors they determine the adjustments in the muscles which maintain normal posture.

The fluid in each of these sacs is kept constantly on the move by the lashing of microscopic protoplasmic hairs on the lining of the sac, forming two vortices. These have a kind of gyroscopic effect in that when we get out of balance, or if we turn round and round quickly, we upset these vortices, causing messages to be sent to the brain to put things right.

An extreme example will drive home this point. A man sitting on his office chair after lunch on a warm day feels drowsy. There is nothing urgent at that moment to claim his attention so he starts to doze. As he does so his chair tips backwards. He awakes just in time to jerk himself and his chair forward, so saving himself from a nasty crash. If he is of an inquiring turn of mind he will wonder what saved him from the fall.

Important elements in this rescue work were the sacculus and utriculus; and we can suppose that it was the necessary violence of the muscular adjustments, due mainly to the speed with which the senses work, that bring such a man speedily to full consciousness.

The sacculus and utriculus are present in the ears of all vertebrates, even in those that cannot hear, such as snakes, which are always said to be deaf. This suggests to some scientists that our inner ear started as a balancing organ and only later took on the additional function of an organ of hearing.

Another component of the inner ear are the three semicircular canals in the form of three tubular loops, two of which are vertical and at right angles to each other and the third horizontal. The fluid in them is continuous with that in the sacculus and utriculus, and they are sometimes thought of as the organs of balance and likened to spirit-levels. In fact they are responsible for detecting acceleration in the sense that they come into play as we move either the head alone or the body as a whole. Each of the tubes has a swelling at one end and in this is a patch of sensory cells like those in the sacculus and utriculus but without the calcareous granules.

The clearest description so far given of the working of these semi-circular canals is by Vitus B. Droscher: when we bend or turn our head the fluid behaves like tea in a cup that is tilted or turned, or

Cephalaspis salweyi, a precursor of modern fishes whose fossils are found in rocks 400 million years old. The cephalaspids, like their direct descendants, the present-day lampreys, had only two semicircular canals instead of the usual three.

carried along. The cup moves, the fluid does not. In the process the sensory cells are slightly bent by the drag of the fluid, and this is registered in the nerves serving them.

In the earliest vertebrates of which we have knowledge, the pre-fishes known as cephalaspids which lived 400 million years ago, the inner ear contained only two semicircular canals, as does that of the present-day lampreys which are descended from them. In the hag-fish, the only living relative of the lamprey, which is degenerate in many other features of its anatomy, there is only one canal, but it has an ampulla at each end, and both these contain a patch of sensory cells. In all other vertebrates there are three semicircular canals, giving a three-dimensional appreciation of space and movement. Because they are exactly at right angles to each other they cater for three types of head movement: horizontal, upright perpendicular and transverse perpendicular.

Our hypothetical somnolescent business man leaning back in his chair after lunch owed his preservation to the sacculus and utriculus and the semicircular canals in his inner ear being connected to an elaborate system of nerves. These go out to the various parts of the brain and spinal cord, so that they are in communication with our conscious and subconscious selves as well as most of our muscles, probably with the eyes as well, since we depend to no small extent on our vision linked with a knowledge of our surroundings to keep ourselves the right way up.

The exact function of the sensory cells and the calcareous granules in our sacculus can best be appreciated by reference to the organ of balance in invertebrates, the statocyst. To understand this we cannot do better than start with what happens in a crab.

Near the bases of the crab's first pair of antennae is a round sac lined with special sense cells and filled with a fluid. Sometimes these sense cells end in tiny filaments projecting into the cavity of the sac. Lying free inside the sac are one or more small calcareous grains, the statoliths. The sac itself is called a statocyst, from the Greek, meaning stationary bladder. The statoliths are secreted by the cells lining the statocyst, and because they are lying loose they will always fall downwards, towards the earth, in response to gravity. The fluid in the statocyst gently brakes their movement. As they touch the sense cells impulses are set up in the nerves and relayed to the brain, and the appropriate muscle movements are set going to keep the crab in the correct position in relation to the pull of gravity.

Some crustaceans, such as the crayfish (*Potamobius*), have two statocysts. Others, like the prawn (*Leander xiphias*), have only one and their balance is not disturbed if this is removed because they possess what is called a dorsal light reaction.

Perhaps the most interesting feature of the crustacean statocyst is that in some species of prawns the lining cells do not secrete the necessary calcareous grains. Instead the animal itself, as we saw earlier, picks up sand grains with its claws and drops these in the statocyst, which has an opening to the exterior. Some of these become glued to the sense-cells and then serve as weights informing the crustacean of the force of gravity. Moreover when the prawn moults the statocyst is shed with the outer covering, so the prawn must pick up fresh sand grains to put into the new statocyst.

Mischievous scientists have from time to time taken a prawn about to moult and put it in an aquarium without sand but with iron filings instead. The deluded prawn, after it has moulted, places some of these in its statocysts, after which the scientist holds a magnet over it. The iron filings are lifted up by the pull of the magnet. The sensory cells are relieved of the weight and the prawn gets the impression that it is upside-down and turns over, so proving what was already obvious, that the statocyst reacts to gravity.

A statocyst not only tells the crab or prawn when it is the right way up, it also gives, like our semicircular canals, information about its other movements in space, as when it turns round. It performs this dual task because there are two types of sensory cells. One is hair-like and hooked and gives information in relation to gravity. The other is long and straight and is mainly affected by movements of the fluid in the statocyst. This swirls around the sensory cells which relay appropriate impulses to the brain.

A statocyst of sorts is present in many other invertebrates and also in fishes. The inner ear of a fish consists of a membranous sac enclosed in a cavity on either side of the rear part of the skull. It has a dual purpose: as the seat of hearing and as an organ of equilibration, the second being probably the more important. The parts concerned more particularly with balance are, as in other vertebrates, the sacculus and utriculus. In sharks the calcareous granules are connected with each other by mucus, but in the bony fishes they are replaced by a single concretion, or otolith. In the sacculus there is one concretion known as the sagitta, in the utriculus there is one known as the lapillus, with a third, known as the asteriscus, in another cavity, the lagena.

These otoliths, or ear-stones, bear patterns of grooves, irregularities and other markings which make it possible for anyone sufficiently expert to say which species of fish a particular otolith came from.

Near the other end of the animal scale are jellyfish, saucer- or umbrella-shaped, with a flimsy, fragile body. They swim by pulsations of the body, like an umbrella being opened and shut. According to circumstances jellyfish can swim horizontally or rise to the surface, turn over and go down deeper or even swim obliquely. A jellyfish has only the simplest nervous system, little more than a nerve-ring round the margin of its bell, and it has few sense-organs. It has a slight sense of touch and a sense of taste. It also has statocysts evenly spaced around the margin of its bell which tell it if it is the right way up.

Statocysts of essentially similar construction are found in many other invertebrates. Most of them have been so little studied that we have to content ourselves with saying they are organs of balance and leaving it at that. There is one big exception, the insects and spiders, as well as related land-dwelling forms such as centipedes, millipedes and scorpions.

Spiders, especially the web-spinners, are the tightrope walkers of the animal world. It is surprising that they do not possess obvious and

well-developed organs of balance. Instead they have very inconspicuous bristles on the legs, arranged in pairs, each pair with its
underlying sensory cell. These have not been fully investigated, but
we know enough about them to say that they may be used by the
spiders to perceive air currents and to help orientate themselves in
their webs.

We can get a general idea how these might work from our knowledge of the organs of balance in insects which have been more fully
investigated. In dragonflies, for example, where the head is attached
to the thorax it engages with tufts of fine bristles that serve as a
gravitational sensing device enabling equilibrium to be preserved in
flight. Dragonflies are relatively primitive, the earliest known being
fossils from the Coal Measures, 300 million years old. In flight they
have an inherent stability, like a glider among man-made machines.
The same is true for insects like craneflies.

Locusts, also relatively primitive flyers, have bristles on the face
that are stimulated by a steady flow of air. They also act as stabilizers.
If the air-flow strikes the locust's face obliquely from one side, the
insect alters the movements of its wings to turn itself into the air
current.

Bristles on the wing surface, acting as organs of touch, enable an
insect to gauge the stresses to which the wing is exposed. In addition,
set in the wing membrane, and especially in the veins, are two kinds
of receptors, the campaniform organs and the chordotonal organs. A
campaniform organ consists of a dome of thin cuticle connected to a
sense cell below. A chordotonal organ consists of a sense cell attached
directly to the undersurface of the cuticle.

A honeybee has a most remarkable eye. It would be untrue to say
it can see the wind, but this is not too far from the truth. Each of its
eyes is made up of 2,500 units, known as ommatidia, which are
hexagonal like the cells in a honeycomb. On the surface of the eye,
set between the ommatidia, are hundreds of very small bristles, so
that the eye looks slightly furry. But these do not interfere with the
bee's vision. These bristles react to each puff of wind, and messages
from them to the brain result in messages going out to the muscles,
bringing the bee back onto its course whenever the wind deflects it.
The effect is much the same as the combination of multitudinous
muscle movements that keep us erect.

A stout-bodied, two-winged fly, like a blowfly, is unstable in the
same sense as a jet plane; in the event of a power failure it would not
glide well. Its hindwings have become modified to a pair of small
balancers, known as halteres. During flight the halteres move up and

down in time with the forewings. Each haltere is a stalked knob rounded at the base where it joins the thorax, and it is jointed to the thorax in the same way as the forewings. Over the rounded base are hundreds of campaniform organs arranged in rows.

So long as the halteres are moving up and down normally there is no strain on the cuticle around the joint. If a haltere is deflected to one side this sets up a strain in the cuticle and the campaniform organs are stimulated. A gyroscope resists any change in the direction of the axis in which it is revolving. A haltere moving rapidly up and down reacts similarly. It is then an alternating gyroscope. If the fly wobbles or inclines to one side the halteres, through their campaniform organs, in conjunction with tactile bristles, the eyes and other sense-organs, act to bring it back on to an even keel.

Tests have been made after snipping the halteres from a fly. Without its halteres the insect dives to the ground when it tries to fly. When a pair of artificial halteres are attached to the stump flying ability is restored, as it is when a cotton thread is attached to the tip of its abdomen, like the tail of a kite, which also produces flying stability.

As well as the chordotonal organs in the wings there are many more in the legs of insects. They probably give the insect information about the positions of the joints, but they are also stimulated by vibrations and are especially prominent in insects like grasshoppers that use sounds to communicate with one another. In the antennae they form what is called Johnston's organ, because it was a man named Johnston who first drew attention to them. Johnston's organ is a group of chordotonal organs that serves to provide information about the position of the antenna at any moment.

Most of the movements of an insect's antenna take place beyond the second joint from the base, the rest of the antenna beyond this being called the flagellum. At the joint between the second segment and the flagellum, Johnston's organ provides information about the movements of the antenna, not only those made when the insect itself moves the antenna but also when the antenna is moved by air currents. Aphides, or plant lice, use this to control their flight, and if the flagellum is cut off the aphid's flight becomes erratic. Normal flight can be restored by fitting the aphid with artificial flagella. The delicacy of the operation involved in giving an aphid a new pair of antennae can best be appreciated by looking at a few aphides on the foliage of a rose bush in the garden. An aphid is little more than 2 mm long and its extremely fine, thread-like antennae are little more than half this length.

The whirligig beetle spends its time swimming on the surface of still water. Ripples can indicate the presence of food or of enemies, so they are important to the beetle. On any fine summer's day we can see a group of these black beetles, each a few millimetres long, swimming round and round on the calm surface of a pond or stream. The beetles weave in and out among one another, searching for even smaller insects that drop onto the water. Although they gyrate in what seems like a confused group they never collide. They are guided by ripples on the water just as flying insects are guided by ripples in the air. Each beetle swims with its antennae in the surface film so that, through its Johnston's organ, it can gauge the curvature, read the message of the ripples, avoid collisions with its fellows, flee from predators or search for food and, aided by its eyes, keep itself in balance with the world around.

The old-time sailor is depicted as licking his finger and then holding it vertically in the air to find out the direction of the faintest breeze. A blowfly goes one better. Before taking off a blowfly raises its antennae to feel the strength of the wind. If it is blowing faster than about 8 km per hour it does not take off. In looking for food, which is putrefying flesh, it must pick up the scent and fly into the wind following the scent trail. When the wind is faster than the speed of the blowfly's air-speed there is no point in taking off.

What is true for insects in flight is true also for wingless insects. Ants have groups of bristles on the neck, on the 'waist' between thorax and abdomen, on the joints of the antennae and on the hip and knee joints of all six legs. These give the most precise gravitational information, so that, for example, an ant going up even a very slight incline knows, from the way the bristles rub on its joints, that it is going uphill and not downhill.

The way in which light falling on an animal operates in keeping the animal the right way up is less obvious except where it possesses what is called the dorsal light reaction. It is one of the simplest reactions to light that are known and is a method of ensuring that an animal retains its upright position. It is found especially in certain aquatic crustaceans. Under normal conditions light falls on the animal from above; so as long as it turns its back to the light it remains the right way up. The light response is mediated through the eye, as can be shown experimentally.

Triops is a primitive fresh-water crustacean, 25 mm long, that looks like one of the extinct trilobites that flourished about 200 million years ago. Its body is covered with a horseshoe-shaped shield towards the front of which is a pair of compound eyes. Between them

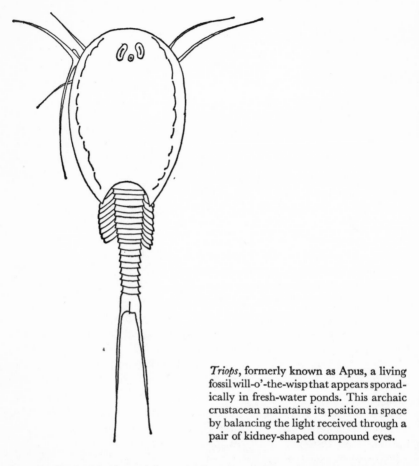

Triops, formerly known as Apus, a living fossil will-o'-the-wisp that appears sporadically in fresh-water ponds. This archaic crustacean maintains its position in space by balancing the light received through a pair of kidney-shaped compound eyes.

is a single simple eye with a window through to the underside of the head. *Triops* keeps its body on an even keel by balancing the light received through the two compound eyes. If one of these is painted over so that no light reaches it the animal swims in spirals. When *Triops* is put in a glass aquarium which is covered above and lighted from below, it turns over and swims upside-down, the movement being started by the simple median eye.

The brine shrimp (*Artemia salina*), another primitive fresh-water crustacean, normally swims upside-down. It rolls into the reverse position when the aquarium is lighted from below. The fish louse (*Argulus*), which normally swims with its back upwards, will turn a somersault to swim upside-down when illuminated from below.

Turn a prawn (*Leander xiphias*) on its side and it rows with its legs in order to bring its back, or dorsal surface, to the light. In this way it rights itself. When placed in an aquarium covered above and lighted from the side, the prawn still struggles to right itself.

The reason for this is that this prawn has another sense-organ to help its equilibration, its statocyst. If this is put out of action, as it easily can be, and we turn the prawn on its side in an aquarium lighted from one side, the prawn stays quietly in this position. Normally the gravity sense in the statocyst and the dorsal light reaction act together with equal force on the legs, keeping the prawn in the upright position. On the other hand, a prawn deprived of its statocyst, standing on a flat surface and out of water, and illuminated from the side, will lean over to an angle of 45 degrees. The sense of contact with the ground and the dorsal light reaction acting in opposition produce a compromise between the upright position and lying on one side.

Fishes known as wrasses (*Crenilabrus*) react in much the same way. When illuminated from the rear in an otherwise darkened aquarium, the wrasse takes a head-up position, making an angle of 45 degrees with the horizontal. When the illumination is from underneath the wrasse swims the right way up because the influence of the organ of balance in the inner ear is stronger than that of light. If the light is from the side its body tips over to the same angle. The inner ear and the dorsal light reaction are acting in opposition to produce a compromise like that seen in the prawn. In this case, also, if the inner ear is put out of action, the wrasse swims on its back when illuminated from below and lies on its flank when lighted from the side.

By some strange quirk, one out of the 30,000 or so species of fishes living today swims permanently on its back. This is the Nile catfish (*Synodontis batensoda*), which has the remarkable habit of swimming slowly at the surface belly uppermost, like a dead fish, but it does not look dead because its colouring is reversed. Its back is silver and its belly coloured. The Ancient Egyptians were sufficiently impressed with it to include it in their murals and sculptures.

It is usual to say the catfish has a ventral light reaction, but how it came to differ from all other fishes we cannot even guess. All we can do is compare this with a similar condition found in some caterpillars. The caterpillar of the clouded yellow butterfly normally lies along the upper side of a leaf stalk. If illuminated from below it will move around to cling upside-down on the underside of the leaf stalk. There are other caterpillars that habitually hang upside-down. They have a ventral light reaction and, as in the Nile catfish, their colouration is reversed.

Caterpillars of the purple emperor butterfly are dark over the front part of the body and light over the rear part, and they habitually hang vertically on leaves, the head uppermost.

Stranger still, there are two kinds of water bugs, both common in ponds. Those of one family, the Corixidae, or lesser water boatmen, swim the right way up in the conventional manner. The others, of the family Notonectidae, or greater water boatmen (now usually known as backswimmers), swim on their backs. Both kinds of water bugs carry a small air bubble between their short antennae. The air

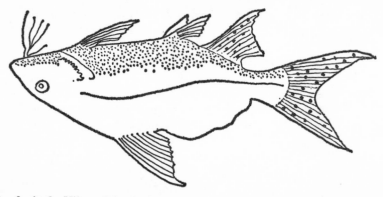

Synodontis, the Nile catfish, also known as the upside-down fish. This fish has long attracted attention by its habit of swimming upside-down. Its only other departure from normality is that its belly is coloured and its back is pale.

bubble bends the antennae away from the head and the stresses set up are detected by sense-organs in the second joint of the antennae. Should we turn a backswimmer over on to its front, the air bubble tends to draw the antennae together. This is detected by the sense-organs in the antennae, and muscular responses turn the insect to its normal position.

In the backswimmer we can see the mechanism for keeping it the right way up—which in its case is upside-down. We cannot see the mechanism for the dorsal light reaction found in so many animals. We can find no trace of a sense-organ and for the moment we can only speculate. Thus many chemical reactions are brought about by light, in the retina of our eye, for instance, or when we take a photograph. If there were light-sensitive chemicals in the skin of an insect, and if the substances they produced when light reached them were to stimulate the nerves, this would be enough. This would be, in effect, a simple form of vision, but without eyes.

The absence of eyes does not necessarily imply an insensitivity to light. For example, in certain mites known as gamasids, parasitic on the skin of larger animals, light receptors are present on membranous flaps associated with the claws of the first pair of legs. These detect the direction of a light source, in a way not yet fully understood, so guiding the parasite to its victim.

Chapter 4

When the world around trembles

Rosie started the New Year badly. On 1st January 1971 Rosie, a young Indian elephant, stopped the circus in Fairfield Hall, Croydon, London. She was taken up in a lift to the second floor, to the circus ring, to do her act, but she ran in before anyone was ready and refused to be led out. For forty-five minutes there was disorder, while attendants tried to keep her from getting among the audience. The only clue to this apparent fit of bad behaviour lay in the report that, as it was ascending, the lift with Rosie in it shuddered.

This unusual behaviour may have been due to an idiosyncrasy on the part of Rosie or it may be that elephants, as a race, are disturbed by tremors, but it recalls how animals react to earthquakes. In 1835, at Concepcion, Chile, at 11.30 hours, horses became disturbed and the dogs all rushed out of the houses. An hour or so before this the sky had been filled with sea-birds, screaming. At 11.40 hours an earthquake shattered the town.

Similar stories have come from other parts of the world at various times, that prior to an earthquake dogs have been heard whining, horses seen trembling, gulls flying around in agitation and chickens showing signs of panic. So far there are no reports of how elephants behave under these circumstances.

We can sympathize with the distraught animals. Even a slight earth tremor can cause anxiety. Some animals at least must be especially sensitive to tremors underfoot since they seem to be alarmed minutes before human beings are aware of what is taking place.

In modern wars sea-birds have shown a remarkable sensitivity to the drone of warplanes. In places that have been regularly bombarded from the air, gulls seem to have associated the sounds of distant aircraft with the explosive noises to come and have heralded these by rising in the air screaming long before human ears could detect the throb of the planes' engines.

It may be that elephants are not specially sensitive to ground tremors and that Rosie's tantrums can be explained otherwise. An elephant with its huge bulk is particularly vulnerable to ground that gives way under its feet. This is exemplified by the behaviour of some elephants being walked from the London Docks through the streets to the London Zoo. When they reached the first pedestrian crossing, with its white and black lines, two of the elephants walked over on black lines and one used a white line. All three tested the line with one foot before walking across. Thereafter, at every pedestrian crossing, the two elephants would use only the black lines, and the one that had tested the white line and found it safe insisted on walking only across a white line.

It is a virtual certainty that every animal is sensitive to vibrations in some form or another, and many grow apprehensive at them. There is a high proportion of species, however, to which vibrations are either an essential of life or enter largely into their code of behaviour.

Among the latter one thinks immediately of snakes which are deaf yet give every sign of being able to hear. This has not yet been fully investigated, but it is generally accepted by those who study them that snakes probably pick up vibrations in the ground through resting their lower jaw on it.

In a different class are the earthworms. Anyone who has kept a pet mole which needs to be fed on earthworms will know the difficulty in getting an adequate supply of worms during a spell of dry weather. The worms go deep down and coil up in the soil, but at night, when the dew forms, they come to the surface and can be seen lying half out of their burrows. Even then it is not easy to catch them. To begin with, a red light must be used because at the first flash of a white light they spring back into their burrows as if an invisible hand were pulling them down. Even then, one must walk with the greatest care as softly as any mouse, and then pounce.

Even more dramatic is the reaction of earthworms to a major disturbance of the earth. Any gardener knows that to push a stick into the earth and wriggle it around will bring earthworms to the surface all around the seat of disturbance. It is usually assumed, probably correctly, that the earthworms are reacting as they would to a mole burrowing.

Moles themselves are highly sensitive to vibrations in the ground. When a mole is at work under its molehill, with the surface of the earth heaving slightly, you can get near to watch if you tread warily. At the first heavy footstep, or if you stumble or kick a pebble, the heaving stops. Provided you avoid these accidents, you may then see the extraordinary sight of earthworms making their exit all around the molehill.

When the world around trembles

Scientists argue, probably rightly, that we ought not to attribute the emotion of fear to animals, especially to the lower animals. We can only retort that when earthworms are escaping from a mole they give every sign of headlong panic. They become positively acrobatic in their efforts to come out onto the surface. And once there they crawl away at a speed far in excess of any they use at other times.

Since a mole feeds mainly on earthworms and may capture anything up to 300 in a day, it is clearly an advantage to its prey to have a built-in reaction to earth disturbances and vibrations. Having once seen the violence of their reaction when a mole is disturbing the earth, one wonders what must happen to earthworms in an actual earthquake!

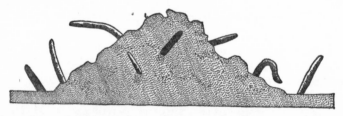

A hill-top drama daily enacted in response to subterranean vibrations. A sure sign that a mole is tunnelling away at the earth beneath a molehill is the appearance of earthworms in a near-panic scramble seeking to escape onto the surface of the ground.

It may be that earthworms react only to certain types of vibration, and that earth tremors are not among them, because it does seem that not all animals are affected in the way the dogs and horses reacted at Concepcion in 1835. There does seem to be selectiveness. For example, when a squirrel is seated 10 m or more up in an isolated tree you can walk around the tree and the squirrel sprawled in the fork will not move a muscle. It can watch you without movement because its eyes have all-round vision. The point is, it is not unduly alarmed at seeing you, so far below. Hit the trunk with the flat of your hand, however, and the squirrel will immediately dive headlong to the ground, with the speed of an arrow. It can only be supposed that the vibrations you have set up in the wood bear some resemblance to the sounds a marten, which feeds largely on squirrels, might make when ascending a tree.

The fact that martens are so rare today that the squirrel may never have seen one is beside the point. These built-in reactions are inherited and persist long after the need for them has vanished.

There is nothing surprising in the squirrel's reaction to your smacking the trunk of its tree. The same thing will happen with perching birds. The wind can make the sapling in which a bird is perched tremble or even sway violently and the bird is, so far as we can see, not at all agitated. But one tap on the stem of the sapling with your finger may be enough to shatter the bird's sleep.

Some years ago a woman who lived in a house 100 m from a lake reported that every time anyone slammed the door of her house fishes jumped out of the water of the lake, and always at the same spot. Fish experts were asked why this should be and all expressed ignorance of it. They had never seen it happen.

In the south of England is a lake beside a main road along which motorized vehicles are passing all day long. Every time a motor-car passes nothing happens. Every time a heavily laden lorry goes by the fishes leap out of the water, and always at the same spot. There must be many neurotic fishes in that lake!

In fact this phenomenon is not uncommon in these days of heavy traffic, but we normally overlook it. Its importance is that it emphasizes how well equipped fishes are to detect vibrations and how much their lives are governed by them.

On each side of a fish, as we can see by looking at one lying on the fishmonger's slab or lying on the kitchen table, is a distinct line running from just behind the head to the root of the tailfin. It is called the lateral line. More careful examination with a magnifying glass, or better still a low-power microscope, would reveal that it continues over the head in three branches.

For a long time the function of the lateral line was in doubt, but now it is fairly well resolved. It is a sense-organ for picking up vibrations. Its structure differs from one kind of fish to another, but in all it works on the same principle. The basic component of the lateral line system is a sense-organ known as a neuromast. This consists of a group of sensory cells and a fine hair-like projection protruding beyond the outer surface of the skin and surrounded by a jelly-like cupule. The projection is, in effect, a kind of hair which responds to pressure. While the fish is at rest and the water around it is perfectly still there is a continuous stream of impulses travelling along the nerve fibres connecting this 'hair' with the central nervous system. Any movement of the hair due to a change in the pressure of water on the cupule causes a change in the pattern of these impulses: their frequency is increased or decreased. This is a message to the brain that there is a change in the surroundings of the fish.

In some fishes the lateral line system may be no more than an open groove with the neuromasts arranged along the floor of the groove. In others the groove is partially roofed over. In the majority of fishes the neuromasts are contained in closed canals which open to the surface by pores. This has been likened to an underground railway with the pores corresponding to the surface stations connected to the deep-lying tube by vertical shafts. This 'underground system' in the lateral line may be filled with mucus or slime. The more primitive the fish the more likely are the neuromasts to be in a simple groove. In deep-sea fishes, living at great depths where the water is virtually always still, the neuromasts are on tiny pimples, or papillae, standing out beyond the level of the skin, presumably to register the slightest vibrations that may occur.

When a fish is moving forward pressure from the water is high in front, on the head. It is low around the head and over the shoulders where the water is flowing more quickly. This is the normal pattern, and so long as it remains this way the impulses in the neuromasts are of a normal pattern. As the fish approaches an obstacle the pressure in front is increased, the cupules are displaced, the pattern of impulses changes and the fish responds by altering course. We see this in action when watching an aquarium. A fish swims towards the glass and at the last minute turns and swims parallel to it, or turns right away.

Any fish or any solid body moving through water disturbs it. The movements of the water are detected by another fish through its lateral line system, and can be interpreted as food, an enemy or another fish of its own kind, and it takes appropriate action. A heavy lorry, producing a minor earth tremor far greater than normal which passes through the water, has a similar effect on the fishes in a lake as the earth tremors at Concepcion had on the dogs and horses. The fishes react by leaping out of the water.

The lateral line system probably also helps a fish in a river to judge between a gentle current and a swift flow, making it seek the bottom away from the main stream when it needs to rest. Although fishes have eyes they need guidance on a dark night from some other sense, and this sense is their lateral line system. Fishes in caves use it. Some fishes living permanently in underground caves are without eyes, but have a more highly developed lateral line system. A fish that becomes blinded can still find its way about, like the blinded ruffe (*Acerina cernua*) that would snap at a glass thread 1 mm thick when this was brought to within 15 mm of its head.

This is a measure of the high sensitivity of the lateral line. If a fish, previously able to see but suddenly bereft of sight, can call upon this alternative sense to achieve such accuracy, and if the vibrations from a slammed door 100 m away can cause other fishes to panic, it would be surprising if this particular sense were not used in all manner of other ways. Indeed from the few other things we know it is probable that for some fishes at least the lateral line system is more important than any other of its senses, that just as we live by sight and a dog lives in a world of odours, so fishes live in a world of vibrations. And this, in fact, is what we find.

Perhaps the first thing we should expect, judging from the effects of the door slamming and the heavy lorry, is that the way to punish a fish would be to ruffle the water around it. In the preliminaries to a fight between two fishes, such as two males fighting over a territory, they indulge in what is called tail-beating. They position themselves alongside each other, a short distance apart, and wave their tails vigorously at each other. We can imagine the effect: it is like two angry men shouting at each other.

In a calmer mood, tail-beating is also used in courtship, the equivalent, we may presume, of a lover whispering endearing words. In human courtship soft words are used to induce closer contact. In fish courtship tail-beating serves to bridge the gap between the two partners which never make physical contact. In such a courtship the male's body quivers and this makes the female lay her eggs, which the male then fertilizes by shedding his milt over them. It is the normal procedure for many fishes to make love without coming into contact and to mate without touching. This describes the courtship of salmon, among others, and a female salmon can be artificially induced to lay merely by beating the water near her rhythmically.

Fishes also have ears, and the lateral line system is a kind of second form of hearing, so the comparisons we have made with love whisperings and angry voices are not too far fetched.

William Beebe, the American zoologist famous for making the first deep descent into the sea, 800 m down in the iron bathysphere, had a particular interest in deep-sea fishes. He tells of his experiments with one of them, a stomiatoid fish which carries its neuromasts on a beard-like barbel hanging from its chin. Beebe found that the minutest movement in the water near the barbel caused the utmost excitement in the fish, which lunged and snapped at the unseen intruder. The fish probably mistook the artificial disturbance for food, which only goes to show how much more it relies for food-getting on its neuromasts than on its eyes.

Gigantactis macronema is a deep-sea anglerfish with a long fishing-line four times the length of its body springing from its nose. This fish has much the same outlines as a pike, which suggests it is capable of swift dashes to seize prey. It has sense-organs on this fishing-line similar to those on the normal lateral line, which detect water movements. When a prey animal is detected some distance away the *Gigantactis* can quickly dash to the end of its own fishing-line to seize it.

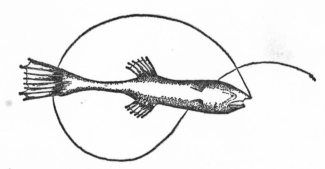

Gigantactis macronema, a deep-sea anglerfish, has two strings to its hunting bow. Anglerfishes catch other fishes with the equivalent of a rod and line, their bait being a luminous lure at the end of a line. *Gigantactis* has a line, or illicium, four times its own length. In the deep-sea darkness it detects prey approaching its lure by vibrations picked up in the illicium.

Fishes swimming in shoals keep in orderly formation, partly by using their eyes to note the position of their neighbours, but also using the pattern of vibrations through their lateral line system. The latter especially comes into use at moments of crisis. Anything disturbing one of the fishes in the rear of the shoal makes it twist and turn violently to make its escape and the vibrations it makes are passed quickly along the shoal so that all fishes in it scramble. The orderly ranks are broken and the fishes dash in all directions, confusing the enemy.

Vibrations of a different kind are used by spiders, through their silken threads. The female garden spider *Aranea diadema* of Europe lays her eggs in a compact cluster in a silken cocoon. When the spiderlings hatch they remain in a cluster for several days, after which they disperse, each building its own small web and starting life on its own. The cocoon is sometimes fastened among the foliage of a shrub or the vine of a creeper. There the newly hatched spiders form a conspicuous yellow cluster, clearly visible to the human eye at 1 m distance, therefore even more noticeable to a bird, with sharper sight than our own, which lands on the shrub or creeper. To insectivorous birds, some of which specialize in eating spiders, a bunch of spider-lings makes an attractive meal.

To counter this vulnerability to predation the spiderlings have a built-in reaction. With the wind swaying the foliage backwards and forwards the spiderlings remain bunched and quiescent. They take no notice of it. Tap the shrub, as when a bird lands on one of its twigs, and the mass of spiderlings begins to heave and expand out-wards as each young spider runs its own way until instead of one mass all are dispersed. Some might be eaten by a bird that had dis-turbed them but others would escape.

As each spiderling moves outwards, on the first dispersal, it lays down a thread of silk. The next time out it can run along this and by laying more silk strengthen it. The more often the spiderlings are disturbed, therefore, the more easily and quickly they can disperse, and the safer they are from attack.

The best known use of vibrations by spiders is in the capture of food. A fly blunders into the web, struggles and shakes it. The spider, usually lurking in a retreat at the edge of the web, perceives the vibrations, rushes out and wraps the victim in silk. The next well-known use is in their courtship, but it is only the web-spinners that use this. The males of most if not all species of spiders possess a sense which enables them to recognize when a female is near without actually seeing her. The hunting spiders that build no web, although they may trail a drag-line of silk, probably recognize a female either by touching with their forefeet a thread she has laid down or by touching the ground over which she has travelled.

How the male web-spinners find the web of the female is some-thing of a mystery. It may be by sheer random searching or by first picking up her silk trail or her scent trail left on the ground beneath her web while she was wandering about choosing the site. When he does find it he telegraphs her. He twangs a thread of the web or he may attach a thread of his own silk to her web and vibrate it. She can tell the difference between the orderly plucking by a male and the irregular agitation of the threads by an ensnared fly. If she is ready to mate she may pluck back at it, in a telegraphic reply. Perhaps we may call it an orchestral love duet. Should she not be in breeding condition he virtually serenades her by vibrating her web, continually doing this until she is ready to receive him.

Less attention has been paid to the finer details of this aspect of spider courtship than to some other fields of animal behaviour. In due course this will, no doubt, be rectified. Then it may prove that the male of every species of web-spinning spider has a particular tune to play, and each female her particular tune to play back to him, and that if they could be played together the result would be a grand string orchestra. It will, however, always be outside the range of human hearing, as are so many vibrations made by animals.

Certainly we can be fairly sure that the patterns of vibrations produced in spider courtship are not random or haphazard, if we may judge from one set of vibrations that has been investigated. Many years ago W. M. Barrows, an American naturalist, investigated the behaviour of orb-web spiders living in his porch. He made an adjustable vibrator, by attaching a fine bristle to the clapper of an electric bell, to find the spiders' behaviour towards vibrations of different frequencies. Large spiders reacted to vibrations with frequencies between 24 and 300 cycles per second (cps), the equivalent of wingbeat frequencies of insects such as house flies. Smaller spiders were found to be sensitive to higher frequencies, between 100 and 500 cps, that is, to the faster wingbeats of smaller insects. Another American found he could entice spiders out of their hiding-places using vibrations of between 400 and 700 cps. Higher frequencies, however, alarmed the spiders and they ran back to shelter or even jumped to the ground. Presumably such vibrations represent danger signals, although it is difficult to think of an enemy that emits such vibrations. It may have been merely a matter of shock, because the spiders reacted in the same way to loud hand-claps.

Most female spiders, the garden spider being an example, lay their eggs, then depart leaving them to their fate. In the case of *Coelotes terrestris*, one of the few spiders in which there is parental care, the spiderlings hatch out in a special nursery, a silken tube. When the mother has caught an insect and is feeding on it she makes the silken funnel vibrate gently in a special pattern, whereupon the spiderlings run to join her at the feast. Should it be against their interests at any time to be away from the nursery, for example if there is danger, she plucks the silk violently, giving an imperative signal for them to return to it—which they obey.

It used to be supposed that honeybees appreciated the same kinds of sounds as we do, indeed that they had their own language of sounds. An old belief had it that if their queen were taken from them the worker bees moaned and wailed, to inform other members of the colony as well as the bee-keeper himself. In return the bee-keeper, if he had worries, would 'tell them to the bees'.

Many attempts have been made by scientists to train bees to come to sugar syrup by using sounds such as whistles and violins. All these have failed. In fact honeybees seem to be quite unmoved by such

European short-eared owl (*Asio flammeus*) in an aggressive
attitude. The 'ears' are tufts of feathers, not hearing organs.

The domestic cat changes its sleeping posture with changes in temperature. Possibly lions do something similar?

A horseshoe crab, or king crab, of the Atlantic coasts of the United States, migrating up the beach.

The stalked eyes of a Malayan sand crab.

The face of a Malayan horseshoe bat (*Rhinolophus luctus*) with the conspicuous horseshoe-shaped nose-leaves.

The common seal *(Phoca vitulina)* probably uses its well-developed whiskers to pick up vibrations in the water.

Tactile hairs on the leg of a grey squirrel are organs of touch for feeling its way among branches.

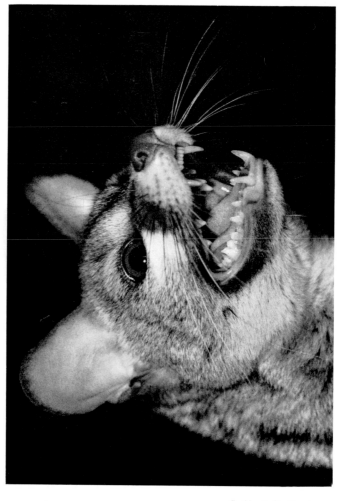

The alert face of an African genet (*Genetta genetta*), including its unusually delicate and sensitive ears.

sounds. Yet there was a strong belief until a few years ago, even among scientists, that bees could hear airborne vibrations, although it had been established as long ago as 1925 that there was nothing in the bees' anatomy corresponding in any way with an ear or any form of auditory apparatus.

Queen honeybees will make a piping sound, and worker bees on the comb will crouch and remain still when she pipes. It seems certain now that there is no question of hearing being involved, and that the workers are responding to vibrations through the comb caused by the piping and picked up by their feet. C. G. Butler and J. B. Free discovered that bees could be attracted to a cocoa tin containing an electric vibrator, vibrating at 50 cps. The old idea bee-keepers had that banging a tin tray near swarming bees made them settle may have had some sense in it.

Another way in which honeybees use vibrations is to repel an invader. When a bee colony is alerted guard bees take up station at the entrance to the hive. At sight of an intruder, such as a robber bee, the guards give out a short sound signal every two to three minutes, which puts all the bees in the hive in an aggressive mood. When danger is past the guards give the all-clear by squeaking, a sound taken up by the workers. Again, it is vibrations the bees are picking up, and an electric buzzer attached to the hive can be used to calm a swarm showing signs of having been disturbed.

Although the use of vibrations is most obvious in the lower animals, there is at least one example of their use by higher animals. The nestlings of birds which nest in trees are hatched blind, their eyes opening some days later. The parents must feed them, and the nestlings must assist by raising their heads and opening wide their mouths, so that the parents can push food down their throats. So long as the eyes of a nestling are unopened it will raise its head and open its beak when the parent lands on the rim of the nest or on a twig near the nest. Anyone finding a nest can make the nestlings do this by tapping the nest or its surroundings.

Once the nestling's eyes have opened it will open its beak only when it sees something moving. This is normally the parent bird, but we can make nestlings gape for food by wagging a finger over the nest.

In this chapter we have examined only a few outstanding examples of animals using a sense of vibrations. Even these make it clear that there is an ill-defined boundary between the vibrational senses and true hearing. Indeed an expert on the subject maintains there is no real boundary. It is, nevertheless, convenient to treat them as if they could be separated, the vibrational senses dealing with vibrations coming through solids or liquids while hearing deals with vibrations in air.

There can be none of these doubts about the lower animals that live in water, the aquatic invertebrates lower in the scale than insects. These, such as jellyfishes, sea anemones, worms and the like, have no organs of hearing or anything remotely approximating to ears, yet they respond to vibrations. Arrow-worms, for example, will turn so that their mouths are directed towards tiny crustaceans swimming towards them. They will do so as efficiently in the dark as in the light. They do so less efficiently when some of the bristles and other bristle-like organs on the surface of their body are damaged.

Some of the bristles are obvious to the naked eye. Others, which are more properly termed rigid cilia, can only be seen with the microscope. It is suspected, from watching the behaviour of some small marine invertebrates, that there may be even smaller 'bristles' that elude the microscope.

Tests show that these various bristles can detect extremely minute vibrations in the water, such as might be caused by a water-flea swimming. Several groups of bristles, in combination, can pick up the direction from which the vibrations are coming. Using them the animal can discriminate between vibrations caused by movements of small prey in the water and the larger current movements and waves in the environment.

Although this function of bristles and cilia has been long suspected it is only in recent years that precise research has been carried out on them. The principle in all instances is of a rigid or semi-rigid rod being deflected, its base then inducting an impulse in a nerve cell. Such results as have been obtained suggest that we may be on the threshold of a major breakthrough in the study of yet another category of sense-organs.

Chapter 5

Our noisy world

It may seem odd that so many authors writing on animal senses should so constantly refer to our own. This is inevitable, not only because more is known about the human sense-organs, but also because it is our primary basis for comparison. Paradoxically it is our own senses that give us an entirely false idea of what is going on in the world around us. We may think of an animal as dumb, merely because we cannot hear the sounds it is making. We may think of it as deaf because it seems to have no ears, yet it may have other means of picking up vibrations. This is because our own sense-organs are severely limited. Were it not so life would be impossible. Nowhere is this more apparent than when we come to consider the ear and the sense of hearing. To appreciate this we need to recall the characteristics of sounds and the details of ear structure.

A barking dog is driving air across its vocal cords, making them vibrate. This sets up vibrations in the air which are received by our ears as sound-waves. Similarly, if we strike a gong, the metal surface moves rapidly back and forth, vibrating, and we can see it do so, but we cannot see the sound-waves it sets up in the air. These strike our eardrums, causing them in turn to vibrate. The eardrum is a thin skin stretched across the passage leading into the side of the head. The real ear is inside. The fleshy flaps or pinnae on each side of the head, which in ordinary speech we call the ears, merely collect the sound-waves and direct them into the real hearing apparatus inside. We could still hear even if we lost our ear-flaps, but less well. We should hear even better if they were larger, as can easily be proved by putting a hand behind one or both ears, as deaf people instinctively do.

The effective part of the ear, lying on the other side of the eardrum, consists of a middle ear and an inner ear. The middle ear is a cavity filled with air, across which runs a chain of three small bones, each the size of a pin's head and known from their shapes as the hammer, anvil and stirrup, or malleus, incus and stapes. The innermost fo these lies against a second opening, set like a window looking into the

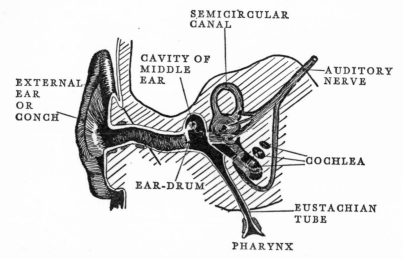

Diagrammatic section through the human ear. Sound waves are directed by the external ear, or conch, into the auditory canal and onto the ear-drum, causing it to vibrate. The tiny ear bones of the middle ear move in response, amplifying the vibrations and passing them on to the inner ear.

inner ear and known as the oval window. This is less than one-twentieth the size of the eardrum.

The inner ear consists of a set of tubes and chambers, embedded in bone harder than anywhere else in the skull, known as the labyrinth and consisting of three semicircular canals joined to a rounded chamber, the utriculus, which communicates with a second chamber, the sacculus, all being filled with fluid. The sacculus leads into that part known as the cochlea, being shaped like a snail's shell, and the oval window is set in the wall of the cochlea.

The hammer and anvil are hinged and the foot of the anvil forms a ball-and-socket joint with the stirrup, the foot of which lies against the oval window. When the eardrum vibrates it moves back and forth no more than 0.00000001 mm. These slight movements cause the chain of bones to move concertina-fashion, so that the vibrations of the drum are repeated in the oval window but amplified twenty-two times, because of the much smaller size of the window as compared with the eardrum.

As the oval window goes in it exerts pressure on the liquid in the labyrinth, and there is yet another membrane, the round window, lying beneath the oval window, which relieves the pressure on the fluid. The vibrations are therefore transmitted to the fluid and the movement of the fluid affects a slender tube coiled in the centre of the cochlea. It is here that the vibrations are picked up by nerves and sent forward to the brain as minute electric currents, which the brain interprets as a pattern of sound.

The ears of all mammals work in the same way. Those of other animals are built on a simpler plan, but by having a general idea how mammals hear we can the better understand how and how much animals can hear.

A dog will pick up very faint sounds. It will hear its master coming down the road before people in the same room can hear anything of him. It will also pick out his footsteps from those of a dozen other people walking along the same strip of pavement.

A dog can also hear sounds we cannot. It can hear a Galton whistle, known as a silent whistle because its pitch is too high for human ears, although young children can sometimes hear parts of it. The human ear can hear sounds from sixteen vibrations a second to between 20,000 and 40,000 vibrations a second, expressed as 40,000 cycles per second or cps. A brief explanation will make clearer the significance of these figures. When we listen to the middle C on a piano we are hearing a sound of 256 cps. The top notes on a piccolo are just over 4,700 cps. Even the figures 30,000 and 40,000 cps are delusory. A child can hear vibrations of 30,000 cps and a child with exceptional hearing can register higher than this, but as we grow older the eardrum thickens so that we hear less and less of the higher notes. An adult of forty years cannot hear more than 20,000 cps, and this figure becomes even less for ages beyond this.

Another way in which a dog's hearing differs from ours is in its better sense of rhythm. A dog can tell if the beat of a metronome changes from a hundred to ninety-six beats a minute. A man can only detect this if he is timing the beats with a stop-watch.

A dog can prick its ears. That is, it can increase their size to collect more sound-waves. There are seventeen separate muscles for moving a dog's ears, whereas we have only nine, and in most people none of these work. So a dog can not only raise and lower its ears but can move them round, to catch sounds coming from different directions. Finally it can shut off its inner ear to exclude sounds, so it can pick out sounds it needs to listen to and concentrate its attention on these. A dog will often appear deaf when we are telling it to do something it has no desire to do, but we have only to whisper the word 'walk' or 'dinner' and its ears will be pricked and its eyes light up immediately.

More experiments on hearing have been carried out on dogs than on any other animal. There have been a few on cats, and these show that their ears work best for frequencies above the range of the human ear but still within the lower range of ultrasonics. It may be that this is why a cat seems to come more readily when a woman calls it, because its ear is more sensitive to the higher notes, nearer to those a mouse uses when it squeaks. A mouse, however, can outdo the cat because it can hear up to 100,000 cps. What we are hearing when a mouse squeaks are only its lower notes. We cannot hear, nor can a cat, the highest ultrasonic notes of the alarm calls by which one mouse alerts another to danger.

All animals so far studied show different ranges of hearing, just as they use different voices. The majority of their calls are beyond the range of our hearing because they are of very high frequencies. The world around us is, therefore, filled with sounds we cannot hear, and what it would mean to us if we could hear them is illustrated by measurements of a bat's ultrasonics, which are far beyond our hearing. Their loudness is measured as 100 decibels, whereas a pneumatic drill, such as is used for road repairs, makes 90 decibels. By the limitations of our senses we are spared an eternal and painful cacophony.

So what we call the peace of the countryside can be, outside our range of hearing, a shattering medley of sounds. Another strongly held illusion has also been shattered, that of the silent oceans, which similarly are filled with a cacophony most of which we cannot hear except with the aid of instruments. This also is a paradox, because the fluid-filled cochlea of our ear, and of mammalian ears generally, is primarily adapted to deal with vibrations through water and it is the intervention of the three little bones, the malleus, incus and stapes, which act as transformers, so enabling us to hear airborne sounds on land. Without these, however, we would be able to go under water and listen to the fishes talking instead.

It was two events in the Second World War that focused attention sharply on the calls of the world underseas. As a protection against surprise submarine attack in 1942, the United States Navy placed listening apparatus on buoys in Chesapeake Bay, to pick up propeller noises. Shortly after these were in position sounds could be heard coming from many directions underseas. Warships went out and saturated the approaches to the harbours with depth charges. All they brought to the surface were large numbers of dead fishes—that had been making the sounds. On the Pacific coast acoustic mines were detonated apparently for no reason—they had been set off by fishes calling to each other.

It had been known for some time that certain fishes make drum-

ming and croaking sounds. The legend of the Sirens, which origin-
ated from the eastern Mediterranean countries and told of sweetly
singing sea-nymphs, is now thought to have been based on sounds
made by the weakfish. The researches made especially by the
United States Navy Department after the events of 1942 have
revealed how widespread are the sounds made by fishes in the sea,
even by certain species of shrimps and prawns. Animals that use
sounds in their courtship or in defence of territory obviously must be
able to hear those made by others of their kind.

Nevertheless fishes, the lowest in the vertebrate scale, have only
imperfect hearing. They have no eardrums and no sign of an ear can
be seen from the outside, but they have an inner ear consisting of a
membranous sac partially constricted into two portions, an upper
chamber, the utriculus, and a lower chamber, the sacculus, with a
small outgrowth from the sacculus, known as the lagena, which
represents the cochlea of the mammalian ear. There are also the
three semicircular canals acting as organs of balance. The utriculus
also acts as a balancing organ, especially in relation to gravity, and
so to some extent do the sacculus and lagena, although they are more
concerned with hearing.

Of the fishes that make sounds, some such as the large ocean sunfish and the horse-mackerel produce them by grating together special
teeth in the throat. In many other fishes there are special muscles or
bones for making sounds, with the swim-bladder acting as a resonator. Some fishes grunt, others growl, or drum, hiss, croon or snore.
These are mainly sounds of low frequency, and fishes are sensitive to
frequencies between 13,000 and 7,000 cps only. They cannot distinguish pitch and they hear in a uniform deep tone in the lower range,
and in the higher parts of their range they hear a uniform high tone.
The sounds they make are monotonous to our ears, but well suited
to their own undiscriminating hearing. On the whole, marine
fishes hear mainly low notes, fresh-water fishes hear mainly high
notes.

There is a story about a monastery in Austria where the monks
were in the habit of ringing a dinner-bell to bring the carp in their
pond together for feeding. If we cannot hear under-water sounds we
can hardly expect fishes to hear airborne sounds. One day somebody
took the tongue out of the bell. A monk went to the edge of the pond
to ring the bell as usual and although no sound came from it the fish
still assembled in their accustomed corner. To test this further the
tongue was put back and a screen was put up at the edge of the
pond. Instead of going to the edge of the pond, where the carp could

see him, the monk went behind the screen. He clanged the bell but the fish took no notice of it. The sound of the bell clearly had nothing to do with the fishes gathering for their meal. It was the sight of the monk that brought them together.

A fish's swim-bladder, which plays so much part in sound-making, can be seen as a limp silvery bag when a fish is cut open for the table. In life it is filled with air and the fish can inflate or deflate it to adjust its own level in the water. In some fishes a row of small bones runs from the inner ear to the surface of the swim-bladder, and this seems to act as an organ of hearing, the bladder acting as a hydrophone as well as a resonator.

The next group of backboned animals, the Amphibia, including salamanders, frogs and toads, seem to be quite unmoved by sounds. They just sit and appear to take no notice. Yet sound and hearing must be important to them, otherwise the different species would not display such a wide range of calls, from a gruff, short croak to sounds like the musical tinkling of a silver bell. Moreover frogs and toads do so much croaking; and one of them croaking will set off all the others. So it is clear they must hear, which is what we should expect from their anatomy. They have an eardrum, which can be seen as a lighter-coloured oval of skin on each side near the back of the head. Moreover this is connected to the inner ear by two bones, one much larger than the other and known as the columella, and the other small and known as the stirrup. The head of the columella touches the centre of the eardrum, and its other end rests against the stirrup, which lies at the entrance to the inner ear.

The strong likelihood is that frogs and toads use hearing mainly when breeding or in relation to the sexual impulse. At other times it seems to be subordinate to other senses. Thus, when we touch a frog sharply in the middle of the back it stretches its hindlegs. This causes it to jump. If we make a noise at the same time as we touch its back the legs stretch more vigorously and the frog jumps even farther. But if we merely make a noise the frog does not jump. It does nothing. We can only assume from this that although a frog has a sense of hearing, other senses, and especially that of touch, are much more important.

Reptiles, except for snakes, have the ear built on a similar plan to that of amphibians, except that it is slightly more elaborate. How much reptiles use hearing is difficult to say. They have the same habit as the amphibians of squatting and apparently taking no notice of noises, although lizards will run away if we hiss at them— not surprising since their chief enemies are snakes. And crocodiles roar quite a lot, especially in the breeding season, and presumably other crocodiles must hear them.

Snakes have no ears, but they respond to vibrations, especially vibrations in the ground, which they can pick up through the bone of the lower jaw. In snake-charming it is not the charmer's music that causes a snake to rear up its head and sway from side to side; it is the sight of the snake-charmer swaying.

Birds are descended from reptilian ancestors and their ears are little different from those of reptiles and amphibians. They have an eardrum and an inner ear, and a columella touches the centre of the drum. The inner ear is slightly more elaborate in that it has a cochlea, but this is not coiled as in the mammalian ear. The majority of birds show no outward sign of the ear; we need to part the feathers to see it. There are occasional exceptions to this, as in the ostrich with its almost bald head and the opening into the ear large and conspicuous. There is, however, no external ear or pinna in birds, yet in spite of this, and in marked contrast to reptiles, birds use a wide range of vocal sounds, and hearing plays an important part in their lives. Experiments show, however, that many birds do not have a keen ear for differences in tone. On the other hand, there are many birds, in addition to parrots and jackdaws, that are excellent mimics of all kinds of sounds, even such complex sounds as the ringing of a bicycle bell.

The barn owl can hunt with deadly accuracy in complete darkness, using only its ears. This has been proved beyond doubt by experiments with a barn owl in a large room made completely light-proof. The floor was covered with dead leaves. The owl would pounce on a mouse running about in the leaves, catching it with its talons, and seldom missing. To prove that it was neither the odour from the mouse nor the heat from its body, a wad of cotton wool was dragged through the leaves. This had no odour nor could it leave a heat trail. Yet the moment the cotton wool was moved, so that it rustled the leaves, the owl pounced and grasped it in its talons.

Owls too are sensitive to sounds above the range of their own voices, which have much the same range as ours. Most birds hear best at the middle of the range of all the tones they utter, but owls can easily pick up the high notes of mice squeaking or of mice rustling among dead leaves, sounds well above the pitch of the owls' own calls. So it is likely that all owls can locate their prey very largely by hearing, but not necessarily with the precision of a barn owl. This is because of their large eardrums, which give a greater area for the reception of sound-waves. Also, although there is only one ear-bone, the columella, it is not set in the middle of the eardrum, as in other birds, but is off-centre. This means that although the columella moves less as the drum vibrates it exerts more force. The drum acts as a lever with its fulcrum at the outer edge. Just as the long handle of a pair of nutcrackers exerts a great force on a nut placed near the fulcrum, so the eardrum exerts a strong pressure on the head of the columella placed off-centre.

The barn owl (*Tyto alba*) can locate and pounce upon a mouse in absolute darkness. Although its ears are hidden under the feathers of the head a barn owl can not only hear the rustle of a mouse in the grass but can locate its position precisely solely by hearing.

The head of an owl is broad compared with the heads of other birds. This sets the ears wide apart, so that there is just a slight difference between the time that sound-waves from a single source reach one ear and the time they reach the other ear. It is this difference in time that enables a pair of ears to pick up the direction of the sound, helped by the asymmetry of the soft parts surrounding the ear, which form a sort of cup leading to the eardrum like the pinna of a mammal. In some owls the cup is larger on one side than on the other. In other owls, it is divided into two compartments, one of which leads to the eardrum, the other ending blindly but also helping in catching sound-waves. A third kind of owl has a flap in front of each ear to deflect the sound-waves and, because these are different in size, the sounds are made to reach the ears at slightly different times.

People often ask over what distance this or that animal can hear, and the question is most often asked about birds. No precise experiments have been made to find out these details and it would probably be useless to try. The distance would depend on the sound made. A bird might hear the sound of an explosion a mile away, yet fail to hear another of its own species singing a quarter of a mile away. And this is true for all animals, ourselves included. We can only suppose that since they lack an external ear the range over which birds can hear, with the possible exception of owls, must be less than that of most mammals.

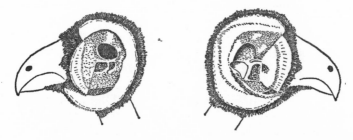

The superb direction-finding of the barn owl is dependent upon the asymmetry of its external ears. Here the two sides of the head are shown, with feathers removed, to show the difference between the receiving cup formed by the external ear on either side. The left ear is on the right of the picture and vice versa.

Even this speculation must be made cautiously. The external ear can give some clue to how keen is the hearing of an animal, because the larger it is the better it can pick up sounds. The African elephant, on the other hand, has the largest ears of any mammal, but the surface is fairly even and its function is to provide for the loss of body heat, the large flapping ears of this elephant being used to cool the rest of the body.

The external ear can bring other advantages. The ears of a horse, donkey or rabbit are constantly being turned this way and that, and the ears can be moved independently of each other. While one is turned to the front the other may be turned to the rear, so the animal can listen in all directions in turn, or can listen in two directions at once. The moment a suspicious sound is heard, however, both ears are brought to bear on it, not only to increase the distinctness with which it can be heard but also, to some extent, to note the direction from which it is coming. This direction-finding may not be so acute as in the barn owl, but it is still fairly efficient.

Some ears, in contrast to the large flat ears of the African elephant, are ornamented with ridges. These correspond to the folds and ridges in our own ears, which were once thought to be useless. Only a few years ago experiments were performed with models of human ears, using earphones similar to a hearing aid. Two results emerged. The first was that if the folds and ridges are flattened out the ears no longer function as direction-finders. The second was that the ridges act as baffles that delay the sound-waves entering the ear, the amount of the delay depending on the angle from which the sound comes. By comparing the difference in the time that it takes a sound to reach the two ears, the brain is able to work out the position of the sound. If it is directly ahead or directly to the rear, there is no delay. If it is from the left it takes longer to enter the right ear, and vice versa.

The ears of some mammals, such as long-eared bats and bush-babies, are folded when the animal goes to sleep, a protection no doubt from having its slumbers disturbed. When the animal is moving about the folds are not completely smoothed out, and it is tempting to suggest these may provide direction-finding baffles, like the ridges in the human ear, especially since they are found mainly in nocturnal animals which would rely largely on hearing.

Another value in having ear-flaps is that they can be turned away from sounds, to shut out harsh noises. Animals, especially those that move about at night and therefore depend on a delicate hearing, will instantaneously turn their ears away from the sound of a motor-cycle backfiring. Bushbabies, as we have seen, fold up their ears while sleeping during the day, when the trees are likely to be filled with noises.

The higher vertebrates, then, depend much on hearing, even those that do not have well-developed ears, and they have them on the head. The invertebrates, with a few exceptions, have no ears, although many have an organ of balance and most are sensitive to vibrations. The exceptions are insects, particularly grasshoppers, crickets and night-flying moths. And they have their ears elsewhere than on the head.

Poets have written about the grasshopper singing all day through the summer, but it does not use vocal music. It is instrumental. Strictly speaking he stridulates, although 'sings' will do for our purpose.

Only the male grasshopper sings, and it is clear from the way the female behaves that it is a love song. The short-horned grasshoppers, which sing by rubbing the thighs of the hindlegs against the edges of the tough forewings, have ears on the body, one on each side, near where the abdomen is joined to the thorax. The long-horned grass-hoppers sing by rubbing their wings together, and have their ears at the base of each foreleg. The ear consists of a drum, a thin membrane stretched across an oval opening in the insect's outer skin or cuticle. Inside is a group of sensory cells, known as the chordotonal organ, and a nerve runs from this to the brain. The insect's ear works, there-fore, on the same principle as our own, although it is vastly more simple. The sound-waves reaching the drum cause it to vibrate, and the vibrations are transmitted through the chordotonal organ to a nerve, and through this to the brain, in the form of nerve impulses.

The short-horned grasshoppers, as already mentioned, sing by rubbing the thighs of the hindlegs against the forewings. If a male and female are put a short distance from each other, and a glass tumbler is put over the male, he can sing his legs off, but the female will take no notice because she is unable to hear him. As soon as the tumbler is lifted, and she can hear his singing, she turns her head and body in a line directed towards him, and then goes forward. The female of the long-horned grasshopper is better at direction-finding because having the ears on the forelegs she can set her ears wider apart, thus increasing the efficiency of her direction-finding.

There are some other insects which have what appear to be ears, yet the way they use them has for long been something of a puzzle. The large yellow underwing moth and the brimstone moth both have a large opening on either side of the abdomen where it joins the thorax. This leads into a cavity lined with a membrane, and on the inside of the membrane are sensory cells and a nerve leading to the brain—so the organ appears to be an ear. And although these insects are sensitive to sounds, they themselves do not make any. For a long time it has been known that these moths will vibrate their wings and run around in an excited manner when a Galton whistle is blown or if a glass stopper is turned in the neck of a bottle, but only within the last few years has it been discovered that the moths' reactions to these sounds are a defence mechanism—against bats, as will be shown in the next chapter.

Other insects make sounds yet do not appear to have special organs of hearing. A number of beetles also stridulate, especially those that burrow in wood or in the ground. The larvae of stag beetles and dung beetles do so. The death-watch beetle strikes its head against the wall of its burrow in the wood, making the well-known tapping, like a watch ticking. This is believed to be a love call, whereas the stridulation of the burrowing larvae of the stag beetles and the dung beetles is believed to be a signal by which the larvae avoid breaking into one another's burrows. If the sounds have a value of this kind then clearly they must be heard by the insects even if no ears can be detected on their bodies.

Plenty of other insects, such as the cockchafers, gnats and bumble-bees, make other noises when flying, but nobody has looked into this to see whether they serve any purpose. Then there are certain cater-pillars, like those of the large cabbage white butterfly, which raise the front part of the body when a whistle is sounded. It is believed that they pick up the sound-waves through the hairs on their body, because when they are moulting, during the short while that the nerves are disconnected from the hairs, they do not react to the whistle.

Hiram S. Maxim, the celebrated inventor, erected a line of electric lamps in New York in 1878, using a transformer to supply the neces-sary current. He noticed that mosquitoes gathered round the trans-former, and that they were all males. He tested mosquitoes with a tuning-fork and found that the males gathered round it. His theory was that they were hearing with their antennae and that the hum of the transformer and of the tuning-fork simulated the hum of the female mosquitoes' wings.

We now know their wings beat 500 times a second, that males can hear the hum up to 25 cm away, that if a male's antennae are cut off he shows no interest in the females and if blobs of gum are placed on his antennae he no longer seeks the female. A further test was to glue a female mosquito by the feet to fine wire so that she could still beat her wings without being able to fly away, out of sight. So long as she beat her wings males flew to her and mated with her. When she no longer fluttered they flew past her as if she were not there.

A most striking result is reported by John R. Pierce and Edward E. Davis Jnr of how a man, impressed by the chorus of crickets in a meadow in New Jersey, made an 'electric chirp maker', the sound from which seemed to him to be a reasonably good imitation of the song of the crickets. When he played this to the crickets they were quite unmoved. He learned later that the chirps we hear from crickets are only low notes incidental to the ultrasonics the crickets listen to and which are produced when they stridulate.

There was a surprising sequel to another piece of 'accidental' re-search in America. On a warm summer's evening in 1956 Kenneth D. Roeder was entertaining friends on his verandah when a swarm of moths came flying around the lanterns. It so happened that one of the guests ran a damp cork round the rim of his wineglass, which gave out the familiar high-pitched musical sound. The moths all dropped to the ground. Roeder's first idea was that they had been paralysed, possibly killed by the sound. The moths were, however, not only still alive but were crawling around over the floor.

Roeder collaborated with a colleague, A. E. Treat, in investigating this—with surprising results. They found the moths had simple ears, which is not news because this was already known. The ears were on each side of the thorax near where it joins the abdomen. The surprise lay in their extreme simplicity.

Each ear is made up of a tympanic membrane behind which is an air-filled cavity and a slender strand of tissue containing only two nerve cells, each sending a fibre to the membrane and, in the other direction, a fibre to the brain. There was a third nerve which does not take part in the hearing and whose function is unknown. Whenever a bat comes within 30 m of one of these moths, its ultrasonic squeaks reach the tympanic membrane of the moth; a message goes through one of the nerve cells to the brain and the moth turns and flies in the opposite direction to the course the bat is following. This is life-saving because the bat cannot locate the moth until within 7 m of it, so it tends to overshoot the mark.

Should the bat swerve in time and come nearer the moth than the 7 m, the second nerve cell sends a message to the brain and the moth closes its wings and drops to the ground.

It is a battle of ears. Sometimes the bat catches the moth, but on 50 per cent of occasions the moth escapes.

The next step was to investigate how the moth can tell the direction in which the bat is flying in order to take appropriate evasive action. The moth's wings join the thorax above and to the front of the ear. The wings are moving up and down, thirty to forty times a second, so the intensity of the sounds reaching the ear is altering rhythmically as on the down-beat the wings absorb the sound and on the up-beat let it through. When the bat is directly behind there is no change in intensity. When the intensity is greater as the wings are raised it means that the bat is in front and below, and so on. Stronger sounds in the left ear mean that the bat is to the left, similarly with the right.

The kangaroo rat lives in the deserts of the south-western United States. It is a rodent with long hindlegs and short front legs, that comes out at night and leaps kangaroo-like over the sand in search of seeds. One unusual feature is that its tympanic bulla, the dome-shaped bone behind the lower jaw that surrounds the middle ear, is greater in volume than the brain itself. Other desert animals have a large bulla and it has long been thought this is linked with an acute sense of hearing.

The eardrum of the kangaroo rat is also large and fairly recent research has shown that its oval window is very small. As a result sounds are magnified a hundred times when they reach the inner ear.

In the same deserts are owls and rattlesnakes, both of which are adept night hunters. The wings of owls are muffled by special downy feathers, but they make a faint whisper with frequencies up to 1,200 cps. Rattlesnakes also are silent hunters, but they make slight sounds just as they are about to strike. These have frequencies of up to 2,000 cps.

Tests with electrodes showed that the kangaroo rat's hearing is most acute between 1,000 and 3,000 cps. Observation showed that kangaroo rats can usually hear both the owls and the snakes and can leap clear a fraction of a second before either strikes.

Malayan pencil-tailed tree mouse *(Chiropodomys gliroides)*
looking out of its home in a bamboo stem, displaying its well-
developed whiskers *(Vibrissae)*, organs of touch.

African white-toothed shrew (*Crocidura manni*) with the typical sensitive and mobile snout equipped with numerous tactile whiskers.

European mole (*Talpa europaea*) eating a worm held under the forefeet, its scent gland exposed on the shoulder.

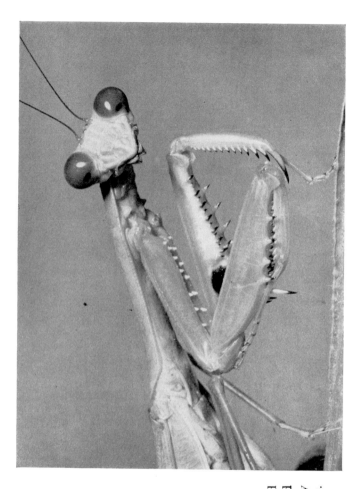

The enormous compound eyes are a marked feature of the predatory praying mantis.

Gymnarchus niloticus, a fish that generates its own magnetic field, using this to find its way around.

A mailed catfish (*Corydoras aeneus*) of South America, with tubular nostrils and barbels, organs of touch, extended.

The Malayan cave bush cricket lives in darkness in the Batu Caves. Its long antennae are its principal sense organs.

Head of the Nile monitor (*Varanus niloticus*) with its forked tongue extended to pick up scent particles.

Chapter 6

Navigating by echoes

Years ago, when a ship's captain wanted to know what depth of water lay under his ship, he would heave the ship to and take a sounding. For ordinary depths a seaman would go to the side of the ship and lower a lump of lead into the water on a line until the lead touched the bottom. Then he would haul it in again. In very deep water, the lead would be on a steel wire wound on a winch, and to take a sounding down to a depth of 4,000 m would occupy two and a half hours. Now, the skipper has only to look at a dial on his depth-recorder, which is a machine that gives a continuous reading of the depth of the sea bed.

All this has been brought about by somebody who had the idea of tapping on the inside of a ship's hull with a hammer and then listening for the echo to come back from the sea floor. Sound travels through water at the rate of just over 1·6 km a second, and by noting the time between the hull being struck and the echo being received back it was a matter of simple arithmetic to find out how deep the sea was at that point. At a depth of 4,000 m the echo would come back in two and a quarter seconds. This rough-and-ready method of taking depths led to the invention of a precision instrument called the echo-sounder, which sends out signals, receives them back and automatically records the depth on a moving roll of paper.

In fact captains of steamers crossing the North Atlantic were using the principle of echo-location long before the echo-sounder was invented. When steaming at night through waters where icebergs might be drifting, they would sound the ship's siren and listen for an echo. If the echo came back quickly it could only be because it was reflected back from an iceberg near at hand.

Bats have been using the same principle for finding their way in the dark for millions of years. Their method is as simple as that used by the ships' captains against icebergs. The bat squeaks and listens for the echo to be reflected back from a solid object. The sooner the echo comes back the nearer the bat must be to a solid object. The solid object might be an insect, and therefore food, or it might be an obstacle which the bat must avoid or break its neck. This method of locating solid objects by the echoes they send back is now known as echo-location. The principle is simple, but the apparatus required to put it into practice is not.

Let us imagine ourselves on the bridge of a ship in mid Atlantic in pitch darkness or in fog. A long blast is sounded on the siren. No echo is heard and confidently the captain gives the signal for full steam ahead. The next moment the bows of the ship crash sickeningly into an iceberg. Because the siren's blast was so long, and the berg so close, the echo was coming back at the same time as the siren was sounding, and therefore our ears were deafened by the siren and we could not hear the echo. The nearer the ship is to a berg the more quickly the echo will return and therefore short blasts must be used. A bat using echo-location must have some means of preventing the sound of its squeaks from reaching its own ears, so that when the echo comes back it is not momentarily deafened. The best way to do this is to shut the ears.

The ability of bats to catch small insects in total darkness at high speed puzzled savants for centuries. When the facts were finally revealed, that bats were navigating and hunting by means of echo-location or sonar, the discovery led to a breakthrough into a whole new world of the use of the senses.

This is what has puzzled everyone for so long. Bats could be seen flying at speed in the half-light and skilfully avoiding every obstacle in their path, yet their eyes were small and it seemed unlikely that they were doing this by sight alone. Because their squeaks were so high-pitched, nobody could hear them, and it did not occur to anyone that they were using the voice.

One evening in London in 1947, at a meeting of a scientific society, there had been a discussion on the use of echo-location for depth-finding in the sea. At the end of it one eminent elderly zoologist rose to his feet and described how he had once watched the ship's captain searching for icebergs by sounding the siren. He added wistfully that if only he had had the wisdom to apply this principle to animals he might himself have discovered much earlier not only the echo-sounder but also the secret of the bat's echo-location.

There had been plenty of opportunity for him and other people to have done this. As far back as 1793 Lazaro Spallanzani, an Italian, caught some bats in a bell-tower, put out their eyes and released the bats in a room in which tapes had been criss-crossed in all directions. The bats had flown among them without once colliding with them. The modern way of repeating this is to blindfold the bat by sticking a bandage over the eyes. The tapes are connected to an electric circuit in such a way that every time one is touched, however gently, an electric lamp flickers.

In the year following Spallanzani's experiments, a French naturalist, Charles Jurine, carried out further tests. He made the discovery that if he plugged a bat's ears with wax so that it could not hear, it blundered helplessly into all obstacles. Spallanzani merely satisfied himself that bats could fly in the dark without using sight. His guess was they were guided by the echo from their wing-beats, an idea which others were to repeat in later years. For example, after the transatlantic liner, the *Titanic*, struck an iceberg and sank with heavy loss of life in 1912, Hiram S. Maxim, the American inventor, tried to invent a safety device for ships. He expressed his conviction that bats were guided by the echoes of low-frequency waves from their wing-beats.

The experiments of Jurine showed that bats were using their ears to find their way about, but no further advances were made until 1920, when H. Hartridge, at Cambridge, noticed bats flying from room to room through a door left ajar, never colliding with it although they had only a narrow space through which to fly. Hartridge concluded that the bats were using sounds of high frequency to guide them. He came very near the truth but failed to press home his studies. A Dutchman, S. Dijkgraaf, also came very near finding the secret in 1932. It was, however, Donald S. Griffin, a young graduate at Harvard, who finally succeeded in 1938.

Griffin had long been interested in bats, especially in their migrations. Several friends suggested he should experiment with bats' ability to find their way in the dark. He heard how Professor G. W. Pierce, of the Harvard Physics Department, had invented the 'Pierce circuit for the stabilization of a radio frequency oscillator by means of a piezoelectric crystal—a simple but ingenious device which is used in almost every radio transmitter to this day'. Pierce had developed the only apparatus then in existence for detecting sounds above the range of the human ear and converting them to sounds the human ear could appreciate.

At first these high-frequency sounds were spoken of as 'supersonic', a word strictly to be used for velocities above the speed of sound. Then came the coining of the new word—new about 1949–50 —'ultrasonics'. The equivalent word for sounds within the range of human hearing is 'sonics'. The use of sonics and ultrasonics in echo-location is called 'sonar'.

Although emphasis is given to the bat's use of ultrasonics it is as well to be clear that bats also use sonics. These are the squeaks we can hear when bats are in their roost. They have frequencies below 30,000 cps, and except for young people most of us cannot hear frequencies as high as 30,000 cps. All the same, ultrasonics is usually taken to mean sounds above 30,000 cps.

When Griffin took a cage full of bats to Pierce's laboratory and held it in front of the horn of the loudspeaker he was thrilled to hear a medley of raucous sounds coming from the bats. However, bats also squeak in the sonic range, and as they moved about the cage their claws scratched the wire-netting, so more careful work was needed to pick out the ultrasonics. Shortly after this, Griffin secured the co-operation of Robert Galambos, a physiologist, and together they carried out the basic experiments which showed how acute is the bats' sonar. They hung curtains of vertical wires in a room 30 cm apart and allowed the bats to fly freely. The number of times they hit the wires was counted. No bat completely avoided collision with them. So long as the wires were 1 mm in diameter the bats avoided them four times out of five; as finer wires were used they collided with them more often, and it was only when wires 0·07 mm in diameter, the size of human hair, were used that they were unable to locate them.

The bats could detect wires down to 0·3 mm even when their ears were being bombarded with ultrasonic noise from loudspeakers on either side of them. They were picking up echoes two thousand times fainter than the noise around them—like someone hearing a whisper through the roar of a football crowd when a goal is scored.

The sounds given out by bats as they are flying range from 10,000 to 100,000 cps, but usually they are between 30,000 and 60,000 cps. If the bat's hearing is not to be upset by the loudness of its own squeaks, so that it would fail to hear the very faint echoes of them, it must shut its ears while the squeaks are being emitted. This it does by contracting a tiny muscle in the ear which pulls the ear-bone, known as the stapes, away from the oval window leading to the inner ear.

That is, it disconnects its hearing. So the bat squeaks, at the same time disconnecting its ear, and as soon as the squeak has gone out the muscle is relaxed and the stapes touches the oval window, and the cochlea is now ready to receive the echo. All the time the bat is flying there is this make-and-break sequence.

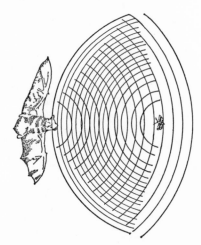

A bat locates an insect by reflected sound waves. The bat squeaks and sound waves go out (lines curving to right; the spacing between the lines represents changing wave-length and frequency of the squeak). Solid objects reflect the waves back, in the form of an echo (lines curving to the left) to the bat's ears.

On a bat-detector, like the machine devised by Pierce, the sounds can be heard as a slow putt-putt, like an idling petrol engine. These sounds are the orientating or searching sounds. As a bat draws near an obstacle, whether a solid object like a branch or one of Griffin's experimental wires, or food in the form of an insect, the squeaks are speeded up. When an insect is only a few centimetres away the rate is stepped up to 200 a second, from the four or five a second used when the bat is merely cruising around. On a bat detector, the sound of a bat chasing an insect crescendoes rapidly from a putt-putt to something like the whine of a band-saw. Having snapped up the insect, the pace is reduced to the four to five per second for cruising and searching until another insect or obstacle is detected, when the squeaks once again rise to a high pitch.

Tests have shown that a bat can detect a fruit fly, one of those tiny winged specks smaller than a pin's head that rise in a cloud from an over-ripe banana, when it is 50 cm or even 1 m distant, or a larger insect 8 mm long at a distance of 2 m.

In the thirty years since Griffin and Galambos brought this extraordinary use of an animal's sense-organs to the notice of the world there have been great advances, but largely in working out the details. These help us to visualize how a bat lives in a world of sounds and echoes as certainly as we live in a world of sights. The echo-location of the long-eared bat is so fine and discriminating that it can fly among the foliage of a tree and pick very tiny insects off the leaves, in the dark, while hovering. Since individual bats tend to hunt in the same air-space, patrolling over perhaps a stretch of road between a hotel and a railway bridge 100 m away, night after night, they must carry an echo-picture of their surroundings, and this must include even fine details. Bats flying in companies, like the serotines and noctules, in picking up the faint echoes on which they depend have to contend with the chorus of sounds their fellows are sending out. This must demand a very fine discrimination, as does the way bats seem to recognize one another by the slight differences in their individual wave-lengths.

In the history of scientific discovery it has happened many times that investigators in different parts of the world have been working on the same problem simultaneously with none of them being aware of what the others were doing. It happened also over the bats' use of echo-location.

Diagram illustrating the essential differences in the use of echo-location by the vespertilionid bats (above) and the horseshoe bats (below). Most bats (above) emit squeaks through the mouth that emerge as pulses. Horseshoe bats (below) squeak through the nose to give a narrow beam, on a constant frequency, which can be swept back and forth like a searchlight.

Griffin, and later Galambos with him, were studying the little brown bat and the big brown bat in America. They began this in 1938, but nothing was published of their work until 1942, by which year everybody was more concerned with the Second World War than with bats. In the meanwhile F. P. Möhres of Germany was reaching similar conclusions about the horseshoe bats. Griffin and Galambos were quite unaware of what Möhres was doing, and vice versa.

The two brown bats of America are small insect-eating bats, and like most other small insectivorous bats they emit their squeaks with the mouth open. Horseshoe bats emit their squeaks through the nose, with the mouth shut. The ultrasonic squeaks of the brown bat take the form of short pulses sent out at frequent intervals. Those of horseshoe bats are explosive pulses sent out at longer intervals. The differences between these bats are linked with the facial feature which gives the horseshoe bats their name. This is the horseshoe-shaped flap of skin on the face. Many bats have similar flaps on the face, sometimes of great complexity, making them hideous to look at. The flaps are known as nose-leaves, and their function was quite unknown until Möhres studied them and showed that they are used to beam the ultrasonic squeaks on an object. Using a comparison with light, we could say that the bat without nose-leaves is striking a match, a horseshoe bat is using a torch. In flight the nose-leaves of a horseshoe bat are continually in motion, bending from one side to the other, concentrating the sounds in a narrow beam of 20° which is swept from side to side of the bat's flight-path. At the same time it moves its ears forwards and back alternately sixty times a second, as direction finders.

The brown bats, and others like them, send out pulses of modulated frequencies which change rapidly from high to low and back again. Those of the horseshoe bat have an almost constant frequency. The full account of what these differences mean to the bats has yet to be worked out.

In the tropics there are fruit bats. They have large eyes and efficient nostrils so have little need of echo-location, either to find their way about or to find their food. They do, however, use a primitive form of echo-location, making clicks with the tongue. Some, which regularly roost in caves in the tropics, use echo-location while in the darkness of the caves but rely on sight when they leave the caves.

For a number of years following the discovery of bats' use of echo-location, there was speculation on how the fishing bats of the tropics operate. These come out at dusk and fly low over the water, dipping down every now and then to fly up with a small fish held in the toes of the hindfeet. They presented a puzzle.

Sound-waves lose much of their energy in passing from air into water, and vice versa. The question was: How could a fishing bat detect a fish under water, since its ultrasonic squeaks would be damped down and echoes from them would be almost entirely lost? Thus, only 0·1 per cent of the sound energy would penetrate the water and any echo from it would decrease by 99·9 per cent as it left the water. The answer was obtained by watching the bats at work. It was found that the bat was able to detect the echoes from a fish only when a part of it broke the surface. Tests in the laboratory showed that a fishing bat would dip down at any ripple and would only grab when a solid object protruded from the water. They could, however, detect a wire of 0·2 mm in diameter projecting 4 mm above the surface.

This explains why fishing bats work in company with pelicans. They catch the fish that break surface while these are fleeing in panic from the pelicans. At other times they catch small fishes from shoals that are being chased to the surface by predatory fishes.

Since this new knowledge about bats has been available all manner of new information has emerged. We used to speak about 'silent oceans'. We now know that the water below the surface is every bit as noisy as the air above it. We are discovering that all kinds of under-water animals have their own methods of making sounds, either for aggression, for finding food or communicating with one another. It is ironic that for well over a century whalers had been telling us that some whales make sounds and nobody had believed them. They actually nicknamed the white whale or beluga the sea canary because of the sounds it made. Research over the past twenty years has fully vindicated the whalers.

About the time that Griffin was hitting upon his great discovery one of his compatriots was planning to build huge concrete tanks which would be filled with sea water and in which dolphins and porpoises would be kept as in a zoo. In due course this man built the first oceanarium in Florida. It was intended more as a public exhibition, but very soon it became a research centre, especially for dolphins.

It soon became apparent that dolphins not only made sounds that people could hear, but that they used ultrasonics as well, and in the various oceanaria that have sprung up since, both in the United States and elsewhere in the world, it is now becoming commonplace to show visitors exactly how specialized the use of ultrasonics is in these animals.

The bottlenosed dolphin, a favourite in the oceanaria, is found to be sensitive to sounds up to 150,000 cps and to emit sounds up to 120,000 cps. The bottlenosed dolphin produces two main sounds, whistling noises and series of rapidly repeated clicks, both on frequencies of up to 170,000 cps. It is the clicks that are used in echo-location and these are emitted more or less continuously.

The behaviour of dolphins in oceanaria has shown that their sonar system is even better than that of a bat. To test this, rubber cups are fitted over the dolphins' eyes, blinding them temporarily. Despite this the dolphins can swim round their tanks at high speed without bumping into any obstacle. They can catch fish thrown into the water for them and one dolphin was able to distinguish between a gelatine capsule filled with water and a lump of fish of the same size. The dolphin ignored the useless capsule, but would always unerringly find the piece of fish.

There are a number of differences between the head of a dolphin and the head of a land animal. First the nostrils are on top of the head and between these and the tip of the snout is an area known as the melon. The ears are different in that the eardrum is connected to the exterior by a ligament instead of a tube and the two ears are not symmetrical, one being farther forward than the other. Presumably this is linked with picking up the direction of sounds.

It is of interest to know that although the dolphins will readily allow the cups to be put over their eyes they refuse to have anything covering the melon. They can, while blindfolded, detect lumps of fish in front of the melon or above it, but fail to find the fish when it is placed under their heads. It has been noticed that the ultrasonics picked up by a microphone are strongest when the melon is pointing directly at the microphone. The conclusion seems to be that it acts in the same way as the nose-leaf of a horseshoe bat in focusing sound into a beam.

In northern South America and Trinidad lives the oilbird, a relative of the nightjar. The belief among some of the local people is that oilbirds contain the souls of criminals, because of their almost human cries as they emerge in the evening from the caves in which they roost by day. It is pitch dark in the caves, and it was inevitable that Donald Griffin, having studied how bats fly about in the dark, should come to Venezuela to study the oilbirds. He found they could find their way about in absolute darkness by emitting steady streams of clicks at frequencies between 6,000 and 10,000 cps. This is well within the range of human hearing and Griffin was able to hear the echoes rebounding from the walls of the caves.

To make quite sure, Griffin trapped some of the birds, filled their ears with cotton wool and found they were then quite helpless in the dark. When the cotton wool was removed they could find their way around and locate their nests normally.

On the other side of the world, from India to the Philippines, are a number of species of swiftlets which also roost in caves. It is from some of these birds that the nests are collected for birds'-nest soup. When swiftlets fly into their pitch-dark caves to roost or to visit their nests they can be heard giving a series of penetrating clicks. These are impulses used for echo-location, but only for detecting obstacles and for navigation in the dark caves.

There is one species of swiftlet, the glossy swiftlet, that lives at the entrances of caves and lacks this ability to use echo-location. When making its nest it carries the nesting materials in its beak, whereas those swiftlets that use echo-location carry the materials with their feet, leaving the mouth free to make the clicks.

There is a strong likelihood that in the years to come many more animals will be found to be using echo-location or to be using ultrasonics in some form or another. Already there is a strong suspicion that rats, several species of mice, hamsters, bank voles, dormice and several other small mammals are either sensitive to ultrasonics or use them in echo-location or for communication. Even marmosets use ultrasonic vocalizations in addition to the squeaks we hear them make. Much of this depends on observed behaviour in relation to high-pitched sounds rather than to precise tests. For example, many of them show characteristic twitching movements of the long whiskers on their snouts or of their large and delicate ears when very high-pitched sounds are made near them. R. J. Pumphrey wrote as early as 1950: 'If you go into a room where rats are kept and talk in an ordinary voice you can see the rats wincing in unison every time you come to a sibilant.' Mice in particular display both the characteristics of twitching whiskers and twitching ears. As for shrews, there have been occasions when young persons with the ability to hear sounds above the normal range of the human ear, so that they can detect the presence of bats when their elders are quite unaware of them, have heard shrews when other people could not hear them. There have also been some tests made on shrews moving about in the dark and avoiding obstacles that suggest they may be using echo-location as part of their navigation in complete darkness.

One species that has been thoroughly tested as recently as 1970 is the long-tailed fieldmouse. It has been set beyond doubt that the babies of this species between six and ten days old, when in distress, as, for example, when separated from the mother, call to her with ultrasonics. She responds by going out from the nest to look for them in order to retrieve them. Exhaustive tests with the necessary apparatus have shown that the mother long-tailed fieldmouse will even stop suckling her babies and leave the nest to carry out searching movements when tape recordings of the infant ultrasonics are played over to her.

Another puzzle has been elucidated in recent years as a consequence of this accumulated knowledge of ultrasonics. This concerns a number of species of moths that were known to make clicking noises as mentioned in Chapter 5. Hitherto nobody could see what purpose was served by these clicks. What we now know is that these moths can hear the ultrasonics of a bat that is hunting them. They have organs of hearing just in front of where the abdomen joins the thorax. Astonishingly they have just two sense cells in each of these organs and these can warn the moth when a bat is on its trail, the moth then taking evasive action by flying away more rapidly or by turning to left or right, or, in the last resort, closing its wings and dropping to the ground. It is a game of touch-and-go in which sometimes the bat wins and sometimes the moth wins.

More surprising still, some moths are able to give out ultrasonic sounds that upset the bats. They do this by rapidly bending and straightening the feet on the hindlegs, where there is a series of scrapers that give out high-pitched sounds in short bursts of 1,000 or more per second, each click containing ultrasonic frequencies within the range of hearing of the bats.

Dorothy C. Dunning has partly tamed bats and trained them to catch mealworms tossed into the air by a machine. Having accustomed them to catching mealworms in mid air she has then played tape recordings of the moths' clicks as a mealworm rose up into the air. The bat diving for the mealworm hears the clicks and swerves away. Presumably the clicks are a warning because these moths were later found to be unpalatable to the bat, so the clicks were acting in the same way as the warning colours of other insects inhibit birds from eating them.

People have often noticed that both penguins and seals seem to be able to find their prey in muddy or murky waters, and there has been speculation as to whether they too are using some form of sonar to do this. The speculation came to a head in 1963 when penguins were seen in the near darkness in San Francisco Zoo retrieving fish that had been thrown into the water for them. A test was later made with four penguins in a tank so constructed that its walls absorbed sound and prevented echoes from the sides of the tank interfering with other sounds. Two fish were thrown into the water. The penguins dived in, but before they hit the water the lights were switched off and more fish were scattered all round the tank. Although the penguins were working in complete darkness they had picked up and eaten all the fish thrown in by the end of thirty seconds.

There is nothing to show that penguins use their voices to produce the necessary train of sounds for their sonar. It is now fairly certain that they are picking up other sounds altogether. When tiny cavities in water collapse they produce clicks, very small, but audible and capable of being picked up on instruments. The rapid movement of penguins causes turbulence in the water which produces these cavities followed by the clicks. So as the animals are moving rapidly about in the water they are causing clicks to be sounded all round their bodies. Their ears pick these up and then pick up the echoes as the clicks are reflected back from the bodies of the fishes. It sounds ridiculous, but apparently is true. Certainly there is no doubt that penguins can catch fish in complete darkness and nobody has yet discovered any other way in which they could do this.

Similar tests carried out with sea lions gave a similar result. The procedure to ensure that there could be no mistake was to throw the fish into a tank in water rendered so murky that the sea lions were working in complete darkness. Then, at a predetermined time after the fish had been thrown in, the sea lions were shepherded out of the tank, using a mesh screen, and the tank was drained and the uneaten fish counted. It was found that the sea lions actually caught the fish more quickly than they did working in daylight. In the dark each sea lion averaged one fish caught every 6·4 seconds compared with 6·46 seconds in daylight. The likelihood is that the faster time in the darkness may have been influenced to some extent by the fish themselves being then at a disadvantage.

Chapter 7

Electric fishes

Every twitch of a muscle is caused by an electrical impulse in a nerve, and in its turn the muscle creates its own electrical disturbance. Every brain wave and every heart beat represents an electrical discharge. Life itself cannot be divorced from electricity, and some animals and all fishes have special electric organs used in defence, for killing prey or as sense-organs.

One of these fishes, an electric catfish, was figured by the Ancient Egyptians on the walls of their tombs as early as 2750 B.C. Another, the torpedo or electric ray, was known to the Ancient Greeks and it was used by the Romans as a cure for gout. This was not because they knew about electricity. Indeed one Roman writer has described the torpedo as giving out a poisonous effluence from its veins that spreads through the water and creeps up the fisherman's line, a dread paralysing force that passes above the surface of the water, creeps down the rod and congeals the blood in the fisherman's hand.

In the late eighteenth century another fish, the electric eel of South America, began to make news, and since then several other species have been found to set up electric fields in recognizable strength. It was, however, a fish with a peculiar tail that led to the most astounding discovery of them all.

The shape of a fish's tail is so familiar and well defined that few of us would have difficulty in drawing it from memory. To describe it in words is naturally more difficult. Nevertheless the outline conjured up in our minds is so clear that we have used the word 'fishtail' to describe a particular form, as in fishtail gas-burner, fishtail wind and fishtail palm. If we take just a casual survey of the scores of different types of fishes known to us we get a very different impression. Indeed taking fishes as a whole, their tails are as varied—often as bizarre—as fishermen's tales.

Ingenious experimenters and those who are mathematically minded have been able to demonstrate satisfactorily that there is a close relation between the shape of the tail and the speed and manner of movement in a given species. There the matter rested until a brief letter appeared in *Nature* in 1961, setting forth the results of some experiments on an African fresh-water fish, *Gymnarchus niloticus*. From these it was seen for the first time that a fish's tail can be put to other uses than pure locomotion.

The fish itself belongs to the family Mormyridae, comprising a number of species found in the rivers and lakes in Africa north of the Equator. In all species of Mormyridae the outward form departs to a fair degree from what we would regard as the normal fish shape. This is more marked in *Gymnarchus niloticus* than in most, however, and its shape is not capable of easy description. The laterally compressed body bears in front a small, pointed head, and just behind the head are the only fins, apart from the soft continuous fin running down the middle of the back and losing itself in a long slender 'rat's tail'. The outline of the body might be called leaf-shaped, recalling the long narrow leaf of the willow, and it ends in a slender backward prolongation recalling to some extent a leaf-stalk. Such an unusual body shape must have constituted a poser to anyone seeking to explain the mechanics of locomotion.

It is well within the competence of even the most non-mathematically minded of us to appreciate that the tail of the typical fish is the main organ of locomotion, the true tail—what the ichthyologist calls the caudal peduncle—being the fleshy narrowing part of the body lying behind the stouter forward portion that houses the body organs. We can also appreciate that the tail fin acts as a rudder, assists stability and plays its part in producing forward movement. If, however, a fish is to swim habitually backwards or forwards, with equal ease in either direction, we should expect some departure from the typical form, though it would not be easy to say what that should be. It would be even more difficult to understand how such a fish could so skilfully avoid obstacles when swimming in reverse.

Gymnarchus has provided the answer to both these problems and in solving them an extraordinary story has been unfolded. Having received a living specimen of *Gymnarchus niloticus* from West Africa, Dr H. W. Lissmann of Cambridge University immersed in the water of its aquarium a pair of electrodes connected to an oscilloscope, whereupon a series of regular impulses were registered on the screen. So the fish was giving out electric pulses. The next step was to immerse the two ends of a copper wire in the aquarium. The fish swam rapidly away, showing apparently the usual escape reactions at the presence of an enemy. The same thing happened when electrical impulses were transmitted to the water. But when its own impulses were fed back to the water, the fish appeared to show the normal reactions to a member of its own species.

The experiments were cut short by the death of the fish and the difficulty of obtaining another for purposes of testing. In the ensuing years, however, Lissmann studied the fish in its natural habitat and in the laboratory. He was impressed with the grace with which it swims, especially with the way it keeps its spine straight and does not lash its tail as most other fishes do. Instead an undulating fin along its back propels it through the water, backwards or forwards with equal ease. Even when turning it maintains this rigid posture, with complex wave-forms running here and there over different parts of the fin at one and the same time. When the fish darts after a small fish, its usual food, it never bumps into obstacles, although its eyes are degenerate and it hunts at night and in muddy waters. Clearly it must have some means of finding its way about.

The tail of *Gymnarchus* had been dissected as long ago as 1847 by Michael Pius Erdl of the University of Munich. In it he found tissue consisting of four thin spindles running along each side to beyond the midline of the body. These he had identified as electric organs.

Early in his studies, Lissmann noticed that when he placed a fresh object in an aquarium containing a *Gymnarchus* the fish would approach it cautiously with what appeared to him to be exploratory movements of the tip of the tail. Suspecting there might be an electric detecting mechanism in the tail he again put a pair of electrodes into the water, connecting them to an amplifier and an oscilloscope, as before. The apparatus recorded a continuous stream of electric discharges at a constant frequency of about 300 pulses per second. This remained unchanged as long as the fish was stationary, but waxed and waned in amplitude as the fish changed position in relation to the electrodes.

Subsequent researches showed that during each discharge the tip of its tail becomes momentarily negative, the head positive. The electric current may thus be pictured as spreading out into the surrounding water in the pattern of lines we get with iron filings and a magnet. The exact pattern of the electric field given out by the fish depends on the conductivity of the water and on the distortions caused by objects with an electrical conductivity different from that of the water. In a large volume of water containing no objects the electric field is symmetrical about the fish. When objects are present, the lines of current will converge on those that have better conductivity than the water and diverge from the poor conductors. Such objects, by distorting the electric field around the fish, alter the distribution of electric potential over its surface, which, if this could be registered, would be a means of detecting objects in the immediate vicinity.

Trying to find how this system worked Lissmann moved a magnet near the glass of the aquarium. The fish responded violently to it as it did also to a comb that had been drawn through somebody's hair, although the electric fields produced by both these could only have been in the range of fractions of a one-millionth of a volt per centimetre.

With his co-worker, K. E. Machin, Lissmann now set to work to train another *Gymnarchus* he had obtained to distinguish between objects that could be recognized only by an electric sense. He used porous pots which themselves had little effect on the shape of the field.

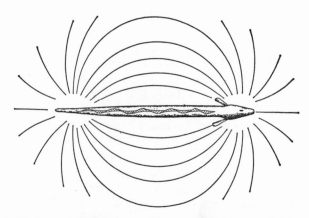

An African fresh-water fish *Gymnarchus niloticus* uses an electric field as a form of radar. This fish can swim backwards or forwards with equal facility. Through its electric field it can also distinguish between friend and foe, food and inedible objects.

The fish was trained to take food from behind the pot which contained water by threatening it with a wire fork every time it approached the other pot, which was a non-conductor, being filled with paraffin wax. It quickly learned to discriminate between the two and would readily swim over to take a piece of food suspended behind the pot filled with water and would ignore similar food behind the pot filled with wax. In other words the two pots, having differing conductivities, were the equivalent of two different colours or shapes to an animal seeking food by sight. A variety of substances were tried in the pots, the result of which was to show quite certainly that the fish could distinguish not only between tap water and distilled water but also between various mixtures of the two.

The mechanism for detecting the electric field lay in the skin of *Gymnarchus*. The tissues and body fluids of fresh-water fishes are good electrical conductors but their skin is not, and in *Gymnarchus* the skin is unusually thick, giving the fish good insulation. In places, especially around the head, pores in the skin lead into tubes filled with jelly through which, presumably, an electric current from the surrounding water can pass. Each tube ends in a small round capsule containing a group of cells and representing an electric sense receptor. Nerves run from these receptors to the brain, in which the areas devoted to the electric sense are very large by comparison with the rest.

The rigid posture maintained by the *Gymnarchus* when swimming is essential if the fish's electric sense receptors are not to be thrown out by movements of the tail, as in ordinary swimming. The body being held rigid keeps the electric field symmetrical with it, so obviating confused information being relayed to the brain. According to Lissmann's tests it seems likely that individual sense-organs may be able to convey information about changes in current as small as 0·003 micromicroampère (a micromicroampère is one-billionth of an ampère) extended over twenty milliseconds. This corresponds to a movement of a thousand singly charged ions. Even the most non-electrically minded can realize that the fish is dealing with electricity in the most exceedingly small quantities.

To sum up, *Gymnarchus* uses its electric field as a mechanism of incredibly fine sensitivity to locate obstacles in its path, whether rocks, vegetation or moving objects, or to find its way into crevices, backwards as well as forwards. Using the same equipment it can also locate prey, be made aware of enemies, even recognize other members of its species, including a potential mate. When two of these fishes approach, even giving out oscillations close in frequency, they shift their frequency. The need for this does not happen often since the range of their electric fields is short. The two would have to come very close to each other to interfere with their respective electric fields, but, like other animals, they resent intruders into their territories. So if two *Gymnarchus* happen to come close to each other a battle of electric currents ensues, the two contestants increasing the frequencies of their pulses, just as two male birds will sing at each other when disputing a territory.

As to enemies, observations in the field show that predatory fishes hunting by sight are inactive at night, while *Gymnarchus* and other electric fishes are inactive during the day, going then into inaccessible hiding-places, often in large numbers. Lissmann found with electrodes connected to a loudspeaker that there was a confusion of ticking, rattling, humming and whistling sounds coming from the rocks and the vegetation of the waters in which *Gymnarchus* and related electric fishes lived, and that with a little practice he could pick out from this bewildering profusion the 'voices' of the various species.

Although it is usual to speak of *Gymnarchus* using radar, this use of an electric field has little in common with it, and it is also fundamentally different from the ultrasonics used by bats. An electric fish does not make use of echoes or of the time period between the impulse and the echo. It is in fact using a sense that is wholly strange to us in which an electrical field provides information by the distortion of its lines. Even the electric lines of force are an abstract idea to us since they cannot be appreciated by any sense we possess, although they can be demonstrated using a magnet and iron filings.

Not only do Lissmann's researches constitute a breakthrough in this particular field, but they make more intelligible the knowledge previously collected about electric organs in other fishes, thus suggesting a possible line of evolution.

The materials from which an electrical apparatus could be formed are already present in an ordinary fish. The electric cells are merely modified muscles and the electric receptors are a modified form of the lateral line system of fishes. Electrogenic or electric-producing organs are found in several marine and fresh-water fishes, which use them in a variety of ways: for stunning their prey by giving an electric shock, for beating off enemies or for finding their way about and locating food in muddy or dark waters. Every time a muscle contracts a tiny electric impulse passes over each cell just before it shortens. In all the electric fishes certain muscles have become modified in such a way that their contractile powers have been lost while their electrical properties have been enhanced.

How the change in the muscle takes place can be actually seen in the course of the development of one of the electric rays, flattened fishes related to sharks. In the young ray the muscle fibres are normal, but as it grows the front end of each muscle fibre balloons out and the nerve endings serving the muscle become concentrated at that front end, while the rear end of the fibres becomes much reduced in size. Each unit constitutes an electroplate. It is surrounded by jelly and contained within a sleeve of connective tissue. The jelly contains fine blood vessels carrying food and oxygen to the

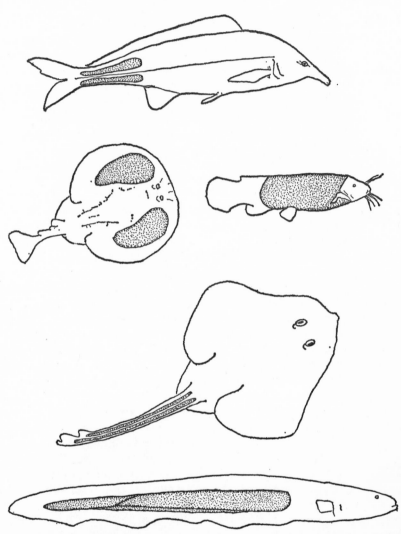

Types of fishes using electric discharges for protection or aggression. (Top) Elephant-snout fish, (centre left) torpedo or electric ray, (centre right) electric catfish, (centre below) skate, (bottom) electric eel. The stippled areas represent the areas of muscle converted to electrogenic organs.

electroplate. The jelly and the connective tissue both serve to insulate the electroplate.

The production of electricity within the organs and its release appear to be similar to that in human muscle, in which the chemical

73

acetylcholine is released at the end-plate of the nerve by the impulse passing down the nerve from the brain. Acetylcholine causes various electrically charged particles, known as ions, to move across the membrane surrounding the muscle fibre and this sets up the electric field. The electroplates in electrogenic organs are not only very numerous but so arranged that their individual tiny voltages (e.g. 0·15 volts) are all added together.

The large stunning shocks are the results of the almost simultaneous discharge of all the electroplates, whilst the regular small pulses used for detecting objects represent a discharge from a few electroplates (usually in parallel) under direct control of the nerve.

It was a puzzle for a long time why electric fishes did not shock themselves. One of the answers lies in the fact that the nerves, especially in the electric eel, are very heavily insulated. The rest of the answers still have to be sought.

The best known of electric fish, the South American electric eel, up to 3 m long is not related to the true eels, although it is eel-shaped. It has very small eyes, its paired fins are very small and it has a conspicuous fin on the underside running from the tip of the tail almost to the throat. The remarkable thing about this fish is that seven-eighths of its body is tail and the electrogenic organs make up 40 per cent of its bulk, the digestive, reproductive and other internal organs being crowded into a small space behind the head. It also swims with its body rigid and in a straight line. This long muscular tail contains electrogenic organs made up of 6,000 to 10,000 electroplates in each of seventy columns running lengthwise on each side of the body arranged like cells in a dry battery. Moreover the electric organ is in three parts, two small batteries and a larger one, and the fish itself is positive towards the head and negative towards the tail. One of the small batteries is believed to fire the large battery which gives out three to six waves at intervals of five-thousandths of a second, each wave lasting two-thousandths of a second and generating 370 to 550 volts, killing animals like fishes or frogs. The South American Indians used to drive horses into the water to bring the eels out of their hiding-places, and the eels' discharge would stun the horses, which sometimes drowned as a result.

The electric catfish lives in fresh waters in Africa; it is 1 m or more long with a plump body and large rounded tail and no fin along the back. It has three pairs of long barbels around the mouth. This was the fish the Ancient Egyptians figured in their tomb paintings three thousand years ago. It can discharge 350 volts, the first discharge being followed by several lesser shocks. The Arabs have used it for electrotherapy since at least the eleventh century, and their name for it is *ra'ad*, the shaker. The electric catfish reacts to magnetic fields and becomes highly sensitive to earth currents that are set up some hours before earthquakes.

Although only the fishes that use electrogenic organs as sense-organs are strictly of interest to us here, a review of the better-known examples of those which use these organs for any purpose, known or unknown, will help our understanding of how the extreme condition seen in *Gymnarchus* could have evolved from that of a normal fish.

A question that has been frequently asked in the past by those who doubt the theory of evolution, even by biologists who do accept the general principles of the theory of evolution—indeed, Darwin himself was puzzled by it—was how could it come about that a fish could suddenly, as it were, acquire a complicated set of electric organs where none existed before? The jump between the one condition and the other seemed almost too much to believe in terms of evolutionary change. We now have a fairly good series showing a gradation from a simple electrogenic organ to the highly specialized organs in *Gymnarchus*. And undoubtedly more species will be discovered in due course to fill in the gaps.

A fairly recent discovery is that skates have electric organs in their tails, although what use they are put to is yet to be found out. They can discharge four volts, and although skates differ from most electric fishes they have similarities with the electric eel in that the nerves serving the electric organs come from the spinal cord and not from the brain.

A close relative of the skate is a fish known as the electric torpedo, which was familiar to the Greeks and used by them for therapeutic purposes. It is a ray, of rounded outline but flattened shape, and the electrogenic organs are large and kidney-shaped, one lying in each of the wide pectoral fins. Whereas the current runs from tail to head in the electric eel and from head to tail in the catfish, in the torpedo it passes from the upper positive side of the fish to the lower negative side. Over a thousand of its electroplates are in parallel, only four hundred are in series, producing forty-five volts. One species, *Torpedo nobiliana*, can electrocute a large fish.

Other rays use an electrical charge of a very much smaller order and for a totally different purpose. These have tiny canals in the skin filled with a jelly-like substance. Should one of them enter estuarine waters where the salinity is changing, a minute change in electrical charge is produced at the boundary between the jelly and the surrounding water. The varying charge produces varying nerve impulses which travel along nerve fibres connected to the inner ends of the canals. These cause the ray to move away from fresh water, or even partially fresh water, and towards sea water.

In Africa and South-East Asia as well as in South America are a number of species known as knifefishes, so called because their bodies are blade-like. They are in fact shaped very much like *Gymnarchus*, but do not necessarily have the same tapered tail and the undulating fin can be on the underside of the body and not along the back. The American knifefishes generate pulses between one and a thousand a second. Some of them produce only one to five pulses per second while resting, merely increasing to twenty pulses when excited; others produce up to a thousand pulses per second. These electric pulses set currents flowing in the water around the fish, the pattern of the current being altered by objects in the surrounding water. Thus animals such as small fish, worms and others, on which knifefishes prey, have a higher conductivity than water so they concentrate the current, thus increasing the flow through nearby parts of the knifefish's body. A rock has a reverse effect. So the knifefish can tell animal from mineral and food from an obstacle.

The situation is not substantially different for the relatives of *Gymnarchus* known as the elephant-snout fishes (family Mormyridae). One remarkable feature of these fishes is that their brain weight is $1/52-1/82$ of the total body weight compared with $1/100-1/200$ in other fish. This large brain may have been evolved in conjunction with the electric organs, since the largest part of it is the cerebellum and hind-brain.

The stargazers are a group of twenty species, looking like gobies, in tropical and subtropical waters of the world. They have heavy heads and large fins. Their eyes are set on top of the head so that the fishes gaze permanently towards the sky. They have small electric organs formed from portions of the eye muscles which can generate fifty volts, enough to make anyone touching the fish throw it aside and wonder what has happened. It is highly probable that the stargazer's electrogenic organs are for defence or for killing prey, but they have not been sufficiently investigated for us to say whether they are used in other ways as well.

Forty years ago W. M. Thornton put forward the hypothesis that deep-sea fishes with their skin so rich in mucus canals must be able to receive and respond to electrical impulses. He did not suggest that they were capable of electrical transmission, rather that the movement of another fish or some other marine animal through the water near by would automatically set up minute electric currents. These he suggested would vary in strength and quality according to the animal that made them, and he implied that the differential would enable the fish to recognize prey from predator. Thornton's ideas cannot be adequately tested until it is possible to bring deep-sea fishes to the surface and keep them alive in aquaria for an adequate length of time. His ideas may be wholly wrong, but, since the whole study of electrogenic organs in fishes is still in its infancy, we may expect in years to come that many more fishes will be shown to use small amounts of electric current in one way or another, including possibly deep-sea fishes.

As if to emphasize this possibility, researches in recent years on a species of prawn showed that it was able to respond to differences in water pressure with changes of only a few centimetres in depth. The surface membranes of all cells are electrically charged and the charges on cells in different parts of the body are often different. When such differences occur on the bodies of animals living in water an electric current flows from one part to the other. In the prawn this extremely minute current is sufficient to cause electrolysis, and an exceedingly thin layer of gas is built up over parts of the body. This minute layer of gas is nevertheless compressible, and the animal's sense-organs can respond to the alterations in its pressure, and thus appreciate differences in absolute pressure in the surrounding water —a novel form of depth gauge and another unsuspected use by an animal of electricity.

Chapter 8

Heat and cold

The domestic cat is descended from the bush cat of Africa. This may, in part, explain why we see it luxuriating in the sunshine and when indoors seeking out the warmest places to sleep, on the radiator, over hot-water pipes, near the open fire in a grate, anywhere indeed where the temperature is high. The cat, always relaxed in sleep, may be cosily coiled up or stretched full out. In 1956 H. Grinsin published an account of how he took temperatures of cats' sleeping places, noted their postures, and found that their sleeping position alters with the temperature of the surrounding air. At the lowest temperatures a cat curls up in what can be called a full circle, with the head and paws tucked together against the belly and the tail wrapped round them. As the temperature rises the cat uncurls to three-quarter circle, then to half-circle, and, finally, to a fully stretched posture.

Children tend to do much the same in bed, curling up in winter and lying spread-eagled, with the clothes thrown off, on a hot summer's night. And cats and children are not exceptions. Everywhere we look we see examples of the way temperature influences or governs the lives of animals. The numbers of species are markedly higher in the tropics than in the polar regions, or even the temperate regions. The distribution of fish species in the oceans closely follows the isotherms. Warm temperatures speed up development, cold temperatures retard it, and this is especially marked in insects. We are more concerned here, however, with the more specialized sense-organs.

One of the more familiar examples, because bee-keeping is of long standing, is the behaviour of honeybees who keep the hive at an even temperature by cooling it when it is becoming too warm and warming it when the temperature inside falls below a comfortable level. On hot days the hive heats up and then most of the workers leave the hive in order that the heat from their bodies should not raise even more the temperature of the interior. Of those that are left a few station themselves in the entrance, facing inwards, beating their wings and drawing the hot air out, the cool air coming into the hive through cracks in its walls. Some may bring in water in their crop and regurgitate it onto the combs to cool them. How they know when to start cooling the hive and when to stop is not precisely known. In winter the bees cluster on the comb and by vigorous movements of their bodies generate heat to warm up the hive.

Ants show a similar attention to their nests and especially to the eggs, larvae and pupae. When the day is warm the worker ants bring these up, carrying them one at a time in their jaws, into the tunnels just beneath the surface which are warmed by the sun. At night they take them down into the bowels of the nest where the heat is retained.

Termites, also social insects like the bees and ants, used air-conditioning long before man had learned to build even a mud hut. Their best-known works are the large termitaria of Africa and Australia, built of mud mixed with saliva, the outer walls of which are concrete hard in the dry season. Inside is a labyrinth of tunnels which, according to those who have studied them, are by their architecture beautifully air-conditioned so far as temperature is concerned, although the percentage of carbon dioxide in the contained air is 5 to 15 per cent, enough to suffocate most animals. The behaviour of the termites themselves also helps the temperature control. The workers, which in a large termitarium 4 m across and 7 m high may number up to a million, cluster in the centre in extremes of heat or cold outside and disperse to the periphery when the sun rewarms a chilled nest or the summer dusk cools an overheated one. The result is that the fluctuations in temperature within the termitarium are far less than in the air outside.

The heat receptors in these social insects are not obvious, but we can see better where they are located in some of the non-social insects, especially the blood-sucking parasites. In the human louse the sense cells are probably scattered all over the body, as it is suspected they are in the bees, ants and termites. They must be fairly sensitive, however, in view of the way lice leave the body of a dead, and therefore cooling, person, or even one in ill-health whose skin has cooled.

A blood-sucking bug, *Rhodnius*, which feeds on warm-blooded animals is guided to its victims by the warmth radiating from their bodies. When these bugs are kept in glass containers and made to go hungry they will walk over to the glass and touch it with their proboscis wherever it has been even slightly warmed by the experimenter's fingers. They fail to do this, or to approach any source of warmth, when their antennae are cut off. It is suspected that certain bristles on the antennae are the heat receptors.

Heat and cold

The bed bug is particularly sensitive to the radiant heat of its victims, apparently being able to detect their heat trails with its antennae while still a metre or more from them. Evidence for this is in their often quoted trick of walking along a ceiling and dropping straight down onto any naked part exposed by a person lying in bed.

The female mosquito also relies to a large extent on her heat-sensitive antennae to find the warm skin of human beings or large quadrupeds, to take the feed of blood without which she cannot produce her eggs successfully. The male, by contrast, sucks plant juices only. The female's antennae are only 3 mm or less long, but she can pick up a source of heat several metres away. She turns her antennae this way and that until the amount of heat stimulus on each antenna is equal, to get the direction of her prospective victim. Then she flies into the wind following the temperature gradient, which merely means that the nearer she gets to the source of heat the stronger the stimulus will be. As she gets closer to her prospective victim she picks up its scent to guide her on the last stage of the journey.

People vary in the amount of heat they give off. Those giving off most will attract mosquitoes to themselves best, and the person who gets excited and throws his arms around, driving up his own temperature, is only playing into the hands of the female mosquitoes in his vicinity. Clothing can also play a part. Dark, and especially black, clothes allow heat to escape more readily into the surrounding air. White clothing reduces the amount of radiant heat. So white clothing helps to keep female mosquitoes at bay.

One of the best anecdotes illustrating the very tiny amounts of heat required to attract small animals is that recounted by Lorus J. and Margery Milne, the well-informed American naturalists. Chicken mites, which are less than 1 mm long, leave the bodies of their hosts at dawn, spending the day in crevices in the woodwork. At night they come out again to seek the bodies of the chickens. In one hen-house there was an electric clock. The small amount of heat it gave out was sufficient to attract them, and they swarmed into it in such numbers as to slow down the working of the clock. At dawn they departed from it and the clock picked up again. The erratic behaviour of the clock, which lost several hours each night, baffled the owner and the clock repairer, until the cause was discovered.

Mites, like everything else, have an optimum temperature for their daily activities. If the temperature is too low they stop work, and they also find temperatures above a certain level uncomfortable. Apparently a chicken's day temperature is above the optimum for chicken mites and their night temperature is just favourable, that is, it represents the optimum for them. Perhaps in this way they avoid being scratched off by the hen or thrown off during a dust bath, and can feed undisturbed while the hen sleeps. Whatever the case may be, their movements are geared to temperature, and they found the electric clock had just the right temperature. And mites have no antennae, so presumably they have heat receptors on their bodies, although these have not yet been investigated.

Fleas also are attracted to warmth, and there are temperature limits which they prefer and which they seek. A flea keeps on wandering at random until it finds these optimum temperature conditions. If it is a cat flea its optimum temperatures will be those of the cat's body. But they only have the urge to seek these temperatures when they are hungry. This is well illustrated by the behaviour of bird fleas. They seek the body of the bird when hungry, then withdraw into the fabric of the nest when satiated.

The bird flea provides an excellent example of how temperature, and an animal's reaction to it, govern the life of a species. When a bird is incubating its eggs and caring for its young all conditions are at their best for the fleas. The optimum conditions are reached: the temperatures for feeding and withdrawal into the nest wall to digest the bird's blood are just as they should be. The fleas can mate and the female lays her eggs under the best conditions. The larval fleas grow rapidly, because the temperature in the nest is at the optimum for this. The optimum in a pigeon's nest, for example, is 37° C., and the pigeon flea's eggs hatch in three to five days. At a lower temperature they may take fourteen days to hatch. So in spring, when the birds are nesting, the fleas flourish and multiply.

However, when the young birds leave the nest only one or two fleas will be carried away on each. The rest will be left behind in the nest. They can then, sometimes, be seen leaving the nest in a swarm, almost certainly to die.

Fleas, mites, bugs and mosquitoes all belong to what are called the cold-blooded animals. That is, the temperature of their bodies is in general about the same as the surrounding air. There are only two kinds of warm-blooded animals, the birds and the mammals, which in general maintain a constant body temperature, no matter whether the temperature of the air around them fluctuates. The warm-blooded animals can control their temperature, lowering it by sweating or panting, or raising it by exercise, by shivering, by eating more, by fluffing out the feathers in the case of birds, or adjusting the hair in the case of mammals.

Heat and cold

It is necessary to qualify these definitions. To take only one example, hawk moths are unable to fly until their body temperature has reached 32–36° C. They do this by fluttering their wings, the muscular action generating heat, as when an athlete warms up before the start of a race. Ringlet butterflies (*Erebia*) that live up on the mountains only come out when the sun is shining. They disappear from sight when the sun goes in. A bumble-bee has its thorax coated with bristles—a fur coat in effect. In the shade its body temperature is 28·7° C. When basking in the sun this rises to 41·6° C. in five minutes, and it falls again rapidly if the sun goes behind a cloud; and if its fur coat is clipped off it cools down much more rapidly.

By contrast, a humming-bird goes each night into a state resembling hibernation. If it did not do so its small body, with such a large surface area relative to its volume, would lose so much heat that the bird would use up its energy reserves and die before dawn. Each night therefore a humming-bird becomes cold-blooded, because its temperature drops to approximately that of the surrounding air.

Because of these considerations it is preferable to speak not of cold-blooded but of poikilothermous animals (with variable body temperatures), and to call warm-blooded animals homoiothermous (with steady body temperatures). This is more an academic point. For everyday purposes it is still convenient to speak of cold-blooded and warm-blooded animals, provided it is kept in mind that there is not this sharp distinction in fact. Both kinds may have sense organs which are heat receptors, and both kinds may have tricks of behaviour, dependent no doubt on their heat receptors, for avoiding the discomfort of extremes of temperature. A good comparison may be made here between lizards and ground squirrels.

In hot deserts the days are hot and the nights are cold. Lizards living in deserts have an elaborate time-table for avoiding the worst effects of these extremes of temperature. They spend the night in a crevice, under a rock or buried in the sand. In such places a certain amount of heat is retained from the day before. Nevertheless by dawn the temperature of the lizard's body will have dropped considerably, so that it is almost stiff with cold. The first thing the lizard does in the morning is to poke out its head to catch the first rays of the sun. The head warms up and the heat then travels around the body. Slowly the lizard thaws out and can crawl into the sun to bask. Each species has a characteristic way of spreading its body and legs to catch the maximum of the sun's rays, and it will from time to time alter this, so that each part of the body gets its turn in warming up.

Even lizards in temperate regions, where the differences between

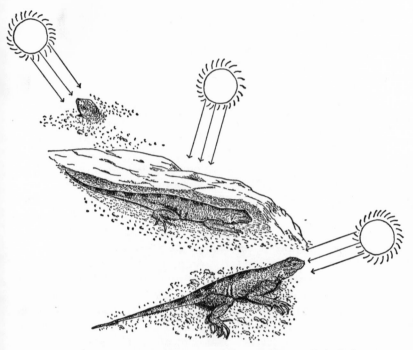

The earless lizard *Holbrookia texana*, of the south-western United States, uses behaviour to keep cool. In the morning the lizard puts its head out of its burrow in the sand to catch the sun's rays. The heat received also warms up the rest of the body and the lizard becomes active. At midday (top) the lizard shelters from the sun's heat. In the afternoon it lies parallel to the sun's rays.

day and night temperatures in spring and summer are not so great as in deserts, adopt these same behavioural procedures.

While basking, the lizard's body temperature rises until it is about 38° C., approximately the same as that of homoiothermous animals. Temporarily at least, the lizard is not cold-blooded in the strict meaning of the word. At this temperature the lizard becomes sprightly and active. It searches for food, defends its territory, seeks a mate and carries out all those activities appropriate to the season.

As the sun rises higher in the sky the rocks or the sand in the desert warm up and the lizard lifts its body off the ground so as not to become overheated. As the midday sun grows hotter the lizard seeks the shade. Later it comes out, and although the strength of the sun's rays is waning they are still hot and the lizard, when not running about, keeps its head pointed towards the sun, to expose as little of its body as possible to the source of heat. As the sun's heat dies down the lizard lowers its body to the ground, which holds the heat longer than the air above it. As night falls the lizard goes into its shelter to minimize the loss of heat from its body by radiation.

Even the homoiotherms do not escape the need for behavioural tricks in relation to temperature, and for comparison with a tropical poikilotherm, the desert lizard, we can choose a temperate region homoiotherm, the antelope ground squirrel of North America. Its habits have been investigated by A. Bartholomew and J. W. Hudson.

In the morning this squirrel comes out of its burrow already warm, so there is no warming-up process, only a little grooming to put its fur straight. Then it goes off to feed, its temperature gradually rising from just below 38° C., when it first left the burrow, to a little above it, about 40·2° C., by noon. Then, with the midday heat, it goes back into the cool of its burrow, and its temperature drops quickly to 38° C. At any time during the heat of the day the squirrel can retire to cool off, but it emerges in the early part of the afternoon to lie in the shade of plants. In mid afternoon comes another period of intense activity and feeding, and as night begins to draw on it returns again to its burrow, its temperature then falling to a little below 38° C.

Grasshoppers and locusts also control temperature by their behaviour. In the morning, when the sun's rays are weak, they turn themselves broadside on to the sun, exposing as much of the surface of the body as possible to its rays, taking up characteristic postures, as lizards do, in order to achieve this. When the sun's heat is strong they turn their heads towards the sun and raise their heads to expose as little as possible to its rays. Many other insects behave in much the same way.

Such variations in the daily activity are governed by small and generalized sense-organs scattered over the body. These have been studied in very few species and are perhaps best known for the human body, and they can be best understood from a few facts known about ourselves. We can map the heat and cold receptors in our own skin by drawing a hot or cold metal point over the surface and marking the spots that respond to it. We find that there are fewer receptors for heat and cold in the human skin than there are for touch, that these lie in different areas, and they are also separate from the touch receptors. The cold receptors, many of which are located near the openings of the sweat glands, consist of bunches of nerve-endings less than 0·5 mm below the surface of the skin. The heat receptors lie slightly deeper and so act more slowly. There are about 150,000 cold receptors in our skin, that is, receptors stimulated only by temperatures below that of the skin. They are more numerous on the forehead, nose, upper lip, chin, chest and fingers than elsewhere. The heat receptors, those stimulated only by temperatures above that of the skin, number 16,000 and are most numerous on the nose, fingertips and near the elbow. The eye is insensitive to heat or cold.

One can but admire the patience of those who provide us with such statistics!

In addition to the sense-cells themselves there is a control, a thermostat, regulating the body temperature. This is in the hypothalamus, a small region on the underside of the brain. Not only is it temperature-sensitive, but messages travel to it from the temperature-receptors in the skin. Through out-going nervous pathways it controls shivering, sweating, panting and the flow of blood under the skin surfaces.

There is some doubt whether the heat receptors of fishes are in the lateral line organs, described in Chapter 4, or in other sense-organs as yet undiscovered. In sharks they may be in the minute jelly-filled pits on the head known as the organs of Lorenzini. That fishes react sharply to heat and cold has been set beyond doubt by numerous laboratory tests. The most striking are, however, those carried out at Harvard University some years ago.

There goldfish were trained to press a lever to allow a small jet of cold water into their aquarium, enough to lower the temperature of the aquarium water by a small fraction of a degree centigrade for each squirt. The goldfish became expert at this and would press the lever as soon as the temperature of the aquarium water reached 33° C. A temperature of 40° C. is lethal to goldfish. The trained goldfish placed at this temperature in experimental aquaria, each fitted with a lever for supplying jets of cold water, quickly set to work and kept on pressing down the lever with their snouts until the temperature of the water around them had dropped to a comfortable level. No fish in the wild state will have such an apparatus available to it. It can only move about until it finds a layer of water in which it is at ease. But the Harvard experiments leave no doubt that at least one species of fish has efficient heat receptors.

Horseshoe bats in temperate latitudes hibernate in caves, but contrary to what has previously been believed they do not sleep continuously from October, when they enter the caves, until the following spring. They are known to move about. They have even been recorded flying from one cave to another thirty-three kilometres away. They do this in response to a drop in temperature at the spot where they are sleeping, and normally this means no more than moving to another spot in the cave where the temperature is at a more comfortable level. In the last few years it has been established that horseshoe bats come out of the caves at times during the winter to feed on dung beetles, which are their favourite food. They do this only when the temperature outside the cave reaches 10° C.

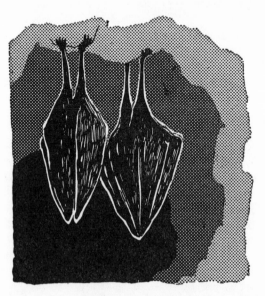

Sleeping horseshoe bats in a cave, with their wings wrapped round the body cloak-fashion. Even when sleeping and hidden within their wings horseshoe bats will shrink from a finger pointed at them at close range, evidence that they are highly temperature-sensitive.

The heat receptors of horseshoe bats must, therefore, be responsive to changes of temperature some distance away while they are in the deep sleep of hibernation.

In some animals there are other temperature responses deeper in the body, from some kind of internal heat and cold receptors the nature of which is at present little understood. Certain strains of domestic rabbit, known as Himalayan, show colour differences according to the temperature at which they are kept. When kept at 28° C. or more they are pure white. At lower temperatures they have black paws, a black nose, black tips to the ears and a black saddle marking. This is entirely due to the temperature of the skin at the time when pigment is forming and the hair is growing. Because of the lower temperature the black pigment, melanin, is formed in the parts mentioned.

It is common for insects bred at lower temperatures than usual to be darker. The best example is in the bug *Perillus bioculatus* which preys on the larvae of the Colorado beetle, the potato pest. At low temperatures there is an increase in its melanin, but it becomes deep red because the orange pigment carotene which it obtains from eating the Colorado beetle larva is deposited in larger amounts than the melanin in its cuticle.

Among the more specialized heat receptors are those possessed by birds and used in incubating their eggs. In the vast majority of birds the feathers covering small areas of the breast fall out at nesting time exposing the bare skin of what is known as the brood patches. There may be one or several brood patches, according to the species. Not all birds have them. The gannet, for instance, has a rich supply of blood vessels in the webs of its feet and these serve the same purpose. The skin and underlying parts of a brood patch are also richly supplied with blood vessels, so the parent bird not only covers the eggs as she sits on them, she also transfers heat to them from her own body. At intervals she turns the eggs over so that they are warmed evenly. When the clutch is large, as in ducks that lay a dozen or more eggs at a time, the parent bird will periodically move the eggs on the periphery into the centre. Moreover in bad weather birds spend less time away from the nest, and are less willing to fly away when disturbed. Clearly, therefore, they must not only be able to warm the eggs but they must have some way of keeping all the eggs at an even temperature. This suggests a heat sense of wider scope than we normally credit them with. Such, for example, as is seen in higher relief in the Egyptian plover.

This bird lays its eggs on the bare ground and buries them in sand during the day to keep the sun off them. Should the sand become too hot the parents go to the nearest river or lake, fill their throats with water, come back and spray the water over the buried eggs.

The peak is reached in the behaviour of the mallee fowl of Australia, a bird that can be said to have a kind of thermometer in its mouth. The mallee fowl is one of a family known as megapodes, or big feet. And if the space devoted to this one species is more than is given to other species mentioned in this book, it is because a fuller account than usual must be given to illustrate the quite remarkable sensory equipment of the mallee fowl.

It is often said that this or that bird or reptile lays its eggs in the sand and leaves them to be hatched by the sun. At best this is only a

87

half-truth. Ostriches which live in semi-desert, for example, must protect their eggs from the sun's heat by sitting on them. Only in this way can the eggs be kept at the correct temperature. If they were left for long exposed to the direct rays of the African sun the eggs would be parboiled.

Nothing animals do to incubate their eggs is ever as simple as it is made to sound. In the case of the mallee fowl of Australia it is highly complicated, although just how complicated was not even suspected a dozen years ago. This is one of the birds known as mound builders. Travellers coming in from the 'outback' told of the huge mounds 5 m in diameter and 1·3 m high. These were at first thought to be burial mounds made by the Aborigines, and it is only just over ten years since the full story has been told.

Mallee fowl, birds as large as turkeys, build a huge mound of sand and vegetable rubbish. The female lays her eggs in the mound and after this the male takes over the main responsibility for their care. The heat of the sun is used, but in a remarkable and deliberate manner, and so is the heat from the rotting vegetation. For eleven months of each year the male mallee fowl is occupied with the preparation and care of the nest. In May the birds dig a large pit in the sand, scraping the earth out with backward thrusts of their large and strong feet and legs. In June, with the onset of the southern winter, they fill the pit with vegetable rubbish scratched together from around it, over a radius of anything up to 50 m. They continue to rake in the dead vegetation until the heap in the pit rises well above the level of the rim. Then come the rains, soaking the vegetable rubbish and making it ferment and heat up. In August the birds begin to mix sand with the decaying vegetation in a smaller pit at the centre of the mound, the actual incubation chamber.

Egg laying begins in September and by this time the mixture of sand and vegetation in the smaller pit has reached a temperature level of 33·5° C. Then the mixture of leaves and sand at the centre is opened up. The male again tests the temperature, and if he is satisfied that it is right he makes way for the hen to lay her eggs. She also tests the temperature, then scrapes away a small part of the mixture and lays an egg in the hole. The male now replaces the mixture in the smaller pit and scrapes the rest of the vegetable material over the mound.

Throughout September and the next three months one egg after another is laid, until finally there is a ring of eggs, standing vertically in the compost. As each egg is laid the birds remove the top of the mould to lay bare the mixture in the smaller pit. Both birds test the temperature, then the hen scratches a hole in which to lay. When she has laid her egg the male closes the incubator pit and replaces the leaves taken from the mound.

The hen lays her eggs at intervals of two days or more. During the intervals the mound is inspected daily, the male doing most of the work, to ensure that the temperature is correct. The hen may lay anything up to thirty-three eggs, each of which takes seven weeks to hatch. So by the time the last egg is laid chicks from the first eggs are already hatching. It also means that the last chicks will not emerge until February or, more usually, March. And all this time the mound is inspected daily and measures taken to ensure a correct temperature.

Should the mound show signs of becoming overheated the mallee fowl simply opens it up to allow the excess heat to escape. If it shows signs of becoming too cool the sun's heat is used to raise the temperature, the mound being opened up until the sun's rays fall directly onto the incubation chamber. At the same time the materials covering it are spread around beyond the rim of the original pit so that they can absorb the greatest amount of heat from the sun before they are replaced.

Since the temperature of the air varies throughout each twenty-four hours and fluctuates to an even greater extent with the seasons, it is a remarkable feat for the mallee fowl to keep it steady all the time.

In all this the mallee fowl is guided by its tongue and the inside of its mouth, which together act as a living thermometer. The birds can be seen picking up a beakful of the materials of the mound, presumably allowing them to touch the tongue and lining of the mouth, and this tells the birds to take the appropriate action, either to heat up or to cool the mounds.

Had the remarkable heat-regulating methods of the mallee fowl not been discovered, pride of place would have been given in this chapter to the performance of the pit-vipers. Their particular sense-organs for detecting heat are even more remarkable than those of the mallee fowl, but there is less discrimination in their use. They demand less of the animal using them.

Pit-vipers include such venomous North American snakes as the moccasins and rattlesnakes. They are named for the two facial pits, each 6 mm deep and 3 mm across, that lie between the nostrils and the eyes. Near the bottom of the pit is stretched a membrane and beyond that is a space which connects with the exterior through a narrow duct. The membrane is shaped like a reflector and in it are 500 to 1,500 temperature receptors in a square millimetre, the number varying with the species. In a rattlesnake there are five times as many heat receptors in one pit as there are on the whole of the human body. It is, therefore, like the retina of an eye, crowded with sense receptors. The overhanging lip at the entrance to the pit casts 'heat shadows' on the membrane and, since the 'fields of view' of the two pits overlap, there is the equivalent of stereoscopic vision, making it a range-finder. Moreover by moving its head from side to side the snake can measure the size of the object giving out the heat. These heat receptors are so sensitive they can respond to changes as small as 0·002° C. and they allow a snake to detect objects only 0·1° C. warmer or cooler than their background.

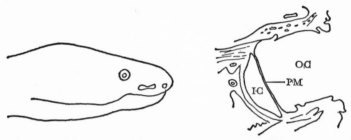

Pit vipers, which include rattlesnakes, can 'see' by radiant heat.
(Left) Head of a pit viper showing the pit containing a heat-detector lying between the eye and the nostril. (Right) Section across the pit. OC = outer chamber, IC = inner chamber, PM = pit membrane.

When these pits were first noticed by scientists they were thought to be an accessory organ of smell or, since snakes have no proper ears, a hearing organ. Another suggestion was that they might be organs for picking up low-frequency vibrations through the air. Then, in 1892, somebody noticed a rattlesnake 'home' on a lighted match. At a later date it was noticed that pythons also have pits on their lips that are sensitive to heat.

The first experiments on pit-vipers in 1937 left no doubt that the pits are heat detectors, and about that time a radiant heat detector was invented which has much in common with the snakes' pits—an interesting coincidence.

To test the value of these pits to the snake several experiments were carried out. Thus a rattlesnake with adhesive tape over its pits was put in a glass cage with a dozen mice. At the end of five days not a single mouse had been touched. Then the tape was taken off the pits and other tape put over its eyes, and the inside of the mouth was sprayed with a chemical that put its sense of smell out of action. This time the snake knew exactly where the mice were, could follow their movements and very quickly caught them.

A pit-viper hunting by day follows its prey by scent, through undergrowth, but relies on its pits finally to locate the prey, even if it is camouflaged. It has an even greater advantage at night when, with its facial pits, it virtually sees its prey by the heat it gives out.

Chapter 9

Mysterious sense of taste

Thirty years ago S. E. Kleinenberg was studying the dolphins in the Black Sea. He wanted to know more particularly what they ate, so he examined the contents of the stomach of any dolphin that was killed. As well as the remains of fish and octopus, which dolphins usually feed on, he found in the stomachs such things as pieces of wood, feathers, paper, cherry stones, even a bouquet of flowers. This is worse than an ostrich, for although this bird is often credited with swallowing literally anything, it usually chooses pebbles and objects in metal and glass. One reason why Black Sea dolphins showed such a catholicity of taste is that they have either no sense of taste at all or so little that it is negligible. An ostrich also has little sense of taste. The human child seems to vie with the ostrich and Kleinenberg's dolphins in putting almost anything into its mouth, quite often swallowing it. Yet it has more taste organs in its mouth when young than it has when adult.

This is only one of the mysteries surrounding what has been called the most mysterious of the five primary senses.

For everyday purposes it is sufficient to say that we smell with our noses and taste with our tongues. In fact, so we are told, what we usually call taste is a combination of a stimulation of the tongue, which is taste in the strict sense, scent stimulation of the nose and pain stimulation of simple nerve-ending in a variety of mucus membranes in the mouth. It is surprising how a simple bodily process can be made to appear complicated—even painful—when subjected to scientific analysis.

We can, however, vouch for the truth of part of this from what unfortunately is a recurrent experience. When a heavy cold blocks the nasal passages and renders the olfactory membrane more or less impotent even the most palatable food tends to lose its charm. An early pragmatic experiment in this field was carried out in the 1920s by a group of diners. They tried eating the excellent food placed before them while holding their noses between finger and thumb. All reported that so long as the nose was held the food was more or less tasteless. They had in fact stumbled on a truth, the explanation for which came later.

Although we talk of a gourmet's palate it is the tongue mainly, in the adult at least, that gives us the sensation of taste, and it is the odour rising from the food in the mouth passing via the cavity at the back of the mouth and into the nostrils that produces the pleasure we experience in eating. We should, in fact, make a distinction between taste, which is experienced via the tongue, and flavour, which is in the nostrils.

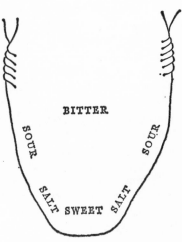

The human tongue seen from above, showing the areas where the four tastes are most easily sensed. The marked areas are where the taste buds are more numerous. The four tastes can also be sensed over the whole tongue but less readily. The human tongue is used here merely as an example. The number and distribution of taste-buds vary from species to species of vertebrates.

Nevertheless, although taste and smell seem inextricably bound together, there is at least one distinct difference between them. We can smell a substance while it is still some distance away. Molecules of odour are carried on the air-stream we draw into our nostrils. To taste the same substance it must be taken into the mouth, must enter into solution in the saliva and this solution must come into contact with certain sensitive cells on the tongue, known as taste-buds.

In a taste-bud is a group, 0·08 mm in diameter, of elongate cells standing on end, the whole sunk in a minute pit in the outer layer of the skin of the tongue. Each cell has a small spike at its outer end, and from each cell a fine nerve passes inwards to join with its fellows before joining up with similar nerves to form the main nerve passing to the brain.

The human tongue has 9,000 taste-buds, pigs and goats have 15,000, a rabbit has 17,000 and an ox has 35,000. Strangely a hare, although like a rabbit in general appearance and feeding habits, has only 9,000, half the number possessed by the rabbit. A bat has 800 and in general vegetarian mammals have more taste-buds than flesh- or insect-eaters.

Not only is flesh more uniform in chemical composition, but carnivores tend to swallow their food whole rather than masticate it. Cats, for example, show no sense of taste for sweet substances. No impulses are registered in their brains when sugar is spread on their tongues. Dogs, of course, will perform tricks for a piece of sugar—but a dog will eat almost anything! Herbivores, on the other hand, must select their food more carefully since they are in great danger of swallowing poisons either inside the plant tissues themselves or on them. They also usually have a 'sweet tooth'. Horses are fond of sugar, and so are mice, except that they soon tire of it.

Taste-buds are arranged in areas, the disposition and extent of which vary slightly with age. There are only four kinds and they can be mapped. In human beings the buds for sweetness are on the tip of the tongue, for bitter taste at the back of the tongue. So wine should be tasted with the front of the mouth, beer at the back. On each side of the front of the tongue are areas sensitive to salty taste and behind these are the sour areas. Only one more thing need be added, that in the human child there are taste-buds on the palate, sides of the mouth and top of the tongue. These disappear with age.

A few years ago L. M. Beidler and R. L. Smallman, at the Florida State University, experimented with putting colchicine on the tongues of rats. This is a substance which inhibits cell division. They found that three hours after an application of colchicine the response of the tongue to chemical stimulation was only 50 per cent of normal. The measurements were made by recording the electrical activity of the taste nerve.

Further investigation, using radioactive tracers, showed that in a normal rat the cells around a taste-bud are constantly dividing, and some of the daughter cells from these divisions go into the centre of the taste-bud to replace cells that are 'worn out'. These replacement cells last only 250 hours, at the end of which time they disintegrate and are replaced. So the colchicine, by inhibiting cell division, was preventing the taste-buds from being replaced, so leading eventually to a loss of taste in the rats.

The investigation and the understanding of the sense of taste are largely a matter of complex biochemistry and much speculation. In 1825 Brillat-Savarin wrote: 'It is not easy to determine exactly wherein the faculty of taste consists. It is more complicated than it appears. Certainly the tongue plays a great part in the mechanism of taste.' As a statement of our knowledge this cannot be bettered today except to say that a few more puzzles, infinitely more problems and several outstanding paradoxes have been exposed.

Why, for example, should very small changes in the shape of a molecule so radically alter the effect a substance has on the taste-buds? The chemical tolylurea can exist in three forms in which the shape of the molecules differ: orthotolylurea, metatolylurea and paratolylurea. The first is tasteless, the second is bitter and the third is sweet. Potassium bromide in a very weak solution is sweet, at twice the strength it is bitter-sweet, at four times the strength bitter and salty and at twenty times it is salty.

Alkaloids are mainly bitter: acids are mainly sweet. A minute and apparently trivial change in the configuration of the molecule can cause a change from tasteless to bitter.

And why should the once popular laxative magnesium sulphate taste merely salty on the tip of the tongue and bitter when it reaches the back of the tongue?

One of the problems concerns how the chemical which impinges on the taste-buds is transducted into electric energy in the taste nerves. It may be supposed that the molecules are absorbed on the surfaces of the cells and that there is a high degree of selectivity in the cell protoplasm, which passes the message to the brain indicating this or that taste. It seems also that the taste nerves themselves also include pathways short-circuiting to the salivary glands and there, according to the shape of the molecules in the food, the composition of the saliva is altered to deal with it. This dual nature of the nerve impulses makes for confusion in any attempt to trace them with micro-electrodes.

What is so extraordinary and unnatural is that the temperature of food increases the taste. (Or is it the flavour? Nobody seems very clear.) An apple warmed by the sun, picked and eaten straight away, is more tasty than one from the same tree eaten soon after but meanwhile made to cool rapidly. It is a simple step from this to the human passion for cooked foods; and the other human preference, for a variety of foods at one meal, is explainable by fatigue.

Taste-buds soon grow tired, which is why a sweet, such as toffee, allowed to remain still in the mouth soon loses its flavour. We have to roll it over, so that it touches other taste-buds, which then register its taste, while the previous taste-buds lose their fatigue and can once more come into play when the toffee is rolled back on to them.

The close link between the sense of taste and the sense of smell is accentuated as we go down the animal scale from the mammals, including man, to the lower invertebrates, and at this latter level the two are indistinguishable. Consequently they are then referred to as a common chemical sense, or chemoreception. Both taste and smell differ from the other primary senses in being chemical, whereas sight, hearing and touch are physical. For that reason scientists prefer to group taste and smell as the chemical senses, and to speak not of taste but of contact chemical sensitivity and of smell as a distant chemical sensitivity.

The need for this distinction can be emphasized by everyday experiences, in which odours characteristic of particular foods may not be those of the foods themselves but the results of atmospheric oxidation of substances present in them. The aroma of roasting coffee beans is far more attractive even than the taste of the coffee. The aroma of frying bacon far exceeds the taste of the bacon, and it must for the moment remain a mystery why the smell of meat stewing is more pleasurable than the chewing of the final product.

These paradoxes may be partially explained by the fact that while in the taste-buds there are only four categories, sweet, bitter, sour and salty, every odorous substance has a different smell, each subtly different from every other, and each is to some extent predictable chemically. Each chemical grouping of atoms makes a characteristic contribution to odour.

To return to the lower reaches of the animal scale, what we call a chemical sense in the lower invertebrates must be relatively simple. Even at the higher levels of animal life, when separate taste and smell organs are present, the act of feeding can have nothing like the range and diversified pleasure we enjoy through our ability to select from a wide range and elaborate by cooking.

The range of chemical substances to which the unicellular animals, such as amoeba, react with their general chemical sense is not great. They move away from any likely to injure their thin cell wall and move towards all others, since these may be edible. A sea anemone will do much the same, except that in it retreating and advancing are a matter of contracting and extending the body. Some animals, such as flatworms, only slightly higher in the scale than sea anemones, appear to have a general sense of taste spread over the whole body.

Earthworms, the next step up in the evolutionary scale, have no specialized sense-organs, only microscopic receptors sensitive to touch, light, vibrations and chemicals, but they seem to have taste receptors grouped in the mouth, judging from the way they show at least slight discrimination in the leaves they pull into their burrows. And yet even this is far from certain.

Earthworms pull leaves and leaf stalks into the mouths of their burrows, especially in late summer and autumn. We see these sticking up from the ground among the grass of a lawn. But an earthworm will just as readily pull the small feathers dropped by birds into its burrow or even, in one instance, short pieces of wool that had been dropped on the grass.

Darwin discussed the way these lowly animals, with such a generalized order of sense receptors, feel the leaves with their lips and turn them around until they are holding them at the point which will make it easiest to drag them into the hole. So whether we can justifiably speak of a precise sense of taste is anybody's guess.

We are on more certain ground in dealing with insects, many of which, such as beetles, plant bugs, cockroaches, bees and caterpillars, are known to have taste organs in the mouth and on the mouth parts. Bees also have them on the antennae, as do wasps and ants. Butterflies and moths, fruit flies and blowflies taste with their feet. A caterpillar given food that is salty or bitter will make spitting movements of the mouth to reject it. A bee can be attracted to sugar syrup. If, having trained it to come to a small bowl of syrup, we

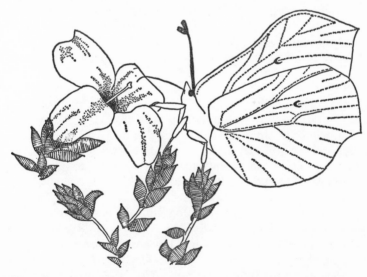

A butterfly samples the nectar of a flower with its feet, which contain its organs of taste. When its feet detect the presence of a solution containing substances agreeable to its taste the long tubular tongue automatically unfolds to sip it. It is sufficient for a single hair on one of the feet to touch the solution to bring the tongue into action.

substitute syrup containing salt or quinine the bee will come to the bowl and will sample the syrup, then reject it. A wasp coming to a smear of jam will first brush it with its antennae, and it has been proved by experiments that bees, wasps and ants can distinguish between distilled water and water sweetened with sugar with their antennae. They will not eat either, however, if quinine (bitter) or acid is added.

People sometimes report having had a butterfly land on their hand and then extend its tongue to lick the skin. Butterflies in the tropics will gather in large numbers to drink salty fluids, such as urine, and presumably the sweat on the hand is equally attractive. If we take such a butterfly and gently hold it by its wings we can carry out a simple test to show that the insect was tasting with its feet before sampling with the tongue. As a substitute for sweat, we can take a sugar solution, dip the end of a fine needle in it and place a minute drop of the solution on one of the butterfly's forefeet. Out will come its long tubular tongue searching for the sugar.

It is the small bristles on the feet that do the tasting, as was shown by V. G. Dethier of the Johns Hopkins University of America. He has described how, with great patience and 'much invective', he rolled a drop of sugar solution up one side of a bristle on the foot of a blowfly and down the other. The insect reacted only when the drop was at the tip of the bristle. Then it put its tongue out.

Further examination shows this simple bristle to have a three-fold function. At its base are three nerve cells, two of which send long filaments up through the bristle, which is hollow, to project beyond its tip. One of these cells comes into action when the tip of the bristle touches a sugar solution, and out comes the tongue. Another comes into action when the tip of the bristle touches a chemical unpleasant to the fly, such as quinine, and the tongue is then withdrawn. The third has nothing to do with taste. It is sensitive to mechanical stimulation, as when the bristle is pressed and bends.

As a consequence of Dethier's researches on the blowfly, more became known about its taste-receptors by 1950 than about those of any other animal, man included. Then, in 1955, J. Y. Lettvin and K. D. Roeder took the work further. They cut off the head of a blow-fly and fixed it by the neck end to a small block of wax. By slight pressure they made the tongue stick out. Then they fitted a very fine glass tube with water over one bristle on the tongue, using a micro-manipulator. A silver wire was inserted into the other end of the tube and this was connected with an amplifier and an oscilloscope. Another silver wire was inserted into the head to complete the circuit.

A single sensory hair (above) on the proboscis of a blowfly. At the base of the hair is a group of three cells, two of taste and one of touch, connected to slender fibres, 0·0001 of a millimetre in diameter, running through the centre of the bristle to a sensitive tip. At the other end the cells connect with the insect's nervous system. (Below) An enlarged view of the three cells.

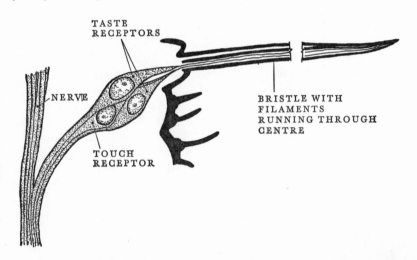

Contact between the tip of the bristle and the fluid in the tube caused the taste nerve to produce a series of electrical impulses which registered as a fleeting trace on the face of the oscilloscope tube, and this was recorded on a film camera. They then put various solutions, sweet and not sweet, in the glass tube and noted what happened.

Lettvin and Roeder found that one of the two taste cells registered for any sweet solutions they put in the tube, and the other registered when non-sweet solutions were put in. Since a blowfly eats especially the sweet substances, non-sweet substances are not acceptable. The third of the cells at the base of the bristle not only acted for touch but also temperature. Altogether, as Lettvin summed it up, one bristle on a blowfly's tongue can test not only the acceptability or non-acceptability of a fluid but also its temperature and its stickiness.

Some of the bristles on the same tongue acted more slowly than others. A very strong concentration would overpower the quickly reacting bristles but not the slowly acting bristles. So between them the bristles could register in the brain of the blowfly a variety of messages, such as 'strong', 'weak', 'too strong', 'too weak', 'acceptable', 'not acceptable', 'very acceptable' or 'very unacceptable', giving a wide range of choice.

A blowfly's feet are five times as sensitive to sugars as its tongue, more so when the insect is hungry. A blowfly starved experimentally for ten days was 700 times more sensitive in its feet than in its tongue. But this seems commonplace for insects. A starved butterfly can detect sucrose (sugar) diluted in water to 0·003 per cent, whereas a well-fed butterfly is unresponsive except to concentrations of at least 0·3 per cent. The human tongue can detect only 0·6 per cent.

A carnivorous water-beetle (*Dytiscus*) was once given a training course, in the usual way, by reward and punishment. When it did what its trainer wanted it was given a piece of meat, sweetened to make it even more attractive. When it went wrong it was given meat treated with quinine. After that, for several months, it was regularly given first salty food, then sweetened meat. When fully accustomed to this routine it was offered not food but a flavour only, in the form of cotton wool containing sugar or salt. It had become so conditioned to 'salt before meals' that it would disregard the acceptable sugar until it had had a chance to reject the cotton wool flavoured with salt.

Honeybees have often been tested for taste. One of the surprising results was that out of thirty-four sugars and closely related substances only nine seemed to be sweet to a bee, although thirty of them were sweet to the human tongue. Indeed most substances which appear sweet to us are apparently tasteless to a honeybee, and whereas most sugars appear sweet to us only those that occur in its natural foods, nectar and honeydew, appear sweet to a bee. Artificial sweetening substances, such as saccharine, are tasteless to a honeybee, and in high concentrations are repellent to it.

In fishes we can make a more positive approach to the problem, despite the fact that there is a primary element of confusion needing to be cleared up. Smell, as we have seen, is a distant chemical sensitivity and taste a contact chemical sensitivity. Imagine a fish with a piece of food a few centimetres from it. The molecules from the food diffuse to the fish through the water to its nostrils, so it smells the food, according to our definition. The same water will also reach the taste-buds, which in fishes are not always confined to the mouth. They may be on the head or on the surface of the body, as in the carp, cod, mullet and sturgeon, or on the barbels, as in catfishes and others. In many fishes the fin-rays are drawn out into long filaments and these sometimes carry numerous taste-buds. The rockling (*Motella*) have free rays in front of the dorsal fin, and these may be rapidly and continuously vibrated for long periods for detecting food, a process that looks singularly like rolling toffee in the mouth.

We can, however, set at rest any doubts about whether a rockling is smelling or tasting the water for food by examining the nerves running away from the taste-buds. In fishes one of the most conspicuous parts of the brain is occupied by the smell centre, the olfactory lobes, and these are supplied by the first cranial nerve, known as the olfactory nerve. The taste-buds are supplied by branches of the seventh (facial), ninth (glossopharyngeal) and tenth (vagus) cranial nerves.

The behaviour of fishes also shows how taste is used. When food was allowed to touch the flanks or the barbels of an American catfish (*Ictalurus*) it quickly turned and seized it. When, experimentally, the nerves serving the taste-buds were severed by surgical operation, the fish took no notice of food applied to these parts.

A red mullet fans the mud with its pectoral fins then explores the bottom it has disturbed with its barbels, in an action recalling the flickering tongue of a snake. The African lungfish has long slender paired fins bearing taste-buds. When one of these touches food the fish swings round and seizes it. Gurnards (*Trigla*) have peculiar pectoral fins in which some of the rays are free and fingerlike, and carry taste-buds. One of these, the gurnard *T. lineata*, apparently walking over the bottom, touches food with one of these free rays, turns and seizes it with its mouth. More important, it may examine it with the rays, as if flavouring it before picking it up with the mouth.

Frogs and toads find their food by sight. A toad once watched an earthworm crawling across the ground. It shuffled its feet to get into the best position for lunging at the earthworm and seizing it in its mouth. It had to use first one forefoot then the other to push the long, wriggling worm into its mouth.

A little time later a baby grass snake wriggled its way across the ground. The toad saw it, watched it for several seconds, shuffled its feet and lunged. It grabbed the grass snake in its mouth, but immediately used its forefeet, first one then the other, in frantic haste to eject the snake from its mouth. A grass snake, when agitated, gives out a repellent fluid from its cloaca.

The adult grass snake feeds on toads. The baby grass snake is identical with an adult except in size, yet the toad, which would have made every effort to escape from an adult snake, readily tried to eat a small replica of it. Its eyes deceived it, but its taste-buds flashed an immediate signal.

These two episodes help us understand the value of having a variety of sense organs.

A parrot shows greater discrimination than most birds. A tame parrot offered food will take it, but will always test it with its tongue before eating it. A parrot kept as a pet in one family for nearly twenty years, during which time it had been given so many pounds of grapes and an equal number of pieces of banana that it must have recognized both by sight, always tested the fruit with its tongue before eating it—and for a good reason. If the banana was not ripe enough or was overripe, or the grapes not of prime quality, it rejected them.

In most birds the tongue is relatively insignificant. That of a parrot is fleshy and large. We would, from first principles, expect a parrot to have a more discriminating sense of taste than most other birds. From the size of its tongue we would also expect it to have more taste-buds, which is true. It has about 400, whereas most birds have only twenty to sixty.

Once again we are faced with the singular fact that a vegetarian animal has more taste-buds than those feeding on flesh or insects, which must be counted as flesh for this purpose.

A rook eats insects, although it will also eat grain, which is why it is unpopular with farmers. It will also eat flesh, and will kill small birds and mice given the opportunity, and will eat carrion. So far as we know a rook has no more taste-buds than usual, which is one-seventh of the number possessed by parrots. Nevertheless a rook tested with a burnet moth gave convincing evidence that it was not without a sense of taste.

The burnet moth is mainly red. Even its greyish forewings are spotted red, and red is one of the warning colours among animals. Insects with warning colours are objectionable. They either have a sting or they are unpalatable. We are told that a young bird may grab in its beak a warningly coloured insect and that it quickly drops it. Thereafter the mere sight of the insect's warning colours is sufficient to deter the bird from taking it in its beak.

This rook, hand-reared from the fledgling stage, was kept in an aviary. It had a hand-reared magpie as companion. Neither bird, we can be sure, had even seen a burnet moth until one day one of this species of moth was handed to the rook, merely to see whether the bird would take it or not. A burnet moth contains prussic acid. The rook took it, but quickly dropped it. Then things began to happen.

The rook stropped its bill on a piece of wood, trying to clean it. It grabbed at blades of wet grass as if trying to cool its mouth. Then it turned on the magpie, chased it around the aviary, trying all the time to attack it, which is something it had never done before.

A rook may have only sixty taste-buds, but this number seems adequate for its needs!

It is well known that many herbivores, especially the hoofed animals, have a special taste for salt and other minerals. They will seek out salty ground or can be attracted by rock salt put down especially for them. The African elephant will dig holes with its front feet searching for salty soil. A camel will seek out plants growing in salty soil. It is not always sodium chloride, the common salt, that they take; they will also show a liking for the metal sulphates, magnesium, iron, copper and nickel. Deer will eat the antlers that they or their fellows have shed and which are lying on the ground. The bongo, the most handsome antelope in Africa, is said to have developed an appetite for charred wood.

Beyond doubt the animals go and lick these things, or chew them, because their bodies are deficient in that particular chemical. This seems to give a clue to another purpose of the taste-buds. They not only tell us that the food we are eating is the right kind of food, they also tell us, in conjunction with some unknown sense somewhere else in the body, that we ought to have this or that kind of food because the body needs it.

Chapter 10

The world of odours

Inside our nose we have a smelling membrane, the olfactory membrane. This is about the size of a small postage stamp. A medium-sized dog has a smelling membrane which, laid out flat, would cover fifty such postage stamps. In our membrane are five million receptor cells. In the best tracker dogs there are 220 million such receptor cells, and each of these works more efficiently than ours. A dog's nose works a million times better than ours.

In 1945 an Alsatian dog used by the Cairo police was called to follow the track of a donkey that had walked across rocky ground four and a half days previously. The dog stopped barking only outside the house where the donkey was found.

To appreciate the Alsatian's performance we can examine what happens each time we put a foot to the ground. Each time the bare foot touches the ground 0·000001 gramme of sweat, the odorous part of which is butyric acid, is deposited. Even when wearing a leather or rubber shoe, billions of molecules pass through the material at each step. The composition of the sweat trace we leave soon begins to change, which is why a dog can tell the direction in which a person has walked after sniffing a trail. A gradient is formed, passing from the oldest to the newest, and a dog can pick up the direction after sniffing over a few metres of trail. Secondly, the molecules slowly sink into the ground so that not only is the composition of the sweat molecules changing, they are sinking into the material of the ground. most readily in loose soil, but rapidly also even in rock.

The Alsatian's performance seems miraculous to us, with our inefficient smelling membrane, but that is only because it is outside our normal experience.

A male moth will find a female moth by the odour she gives out. His olfactory receptors are in his antennae which are feather-like and, compared with the size of his body, large. The female moth, newly emerged from the cocoon and not yet ready to mate, gives out no scent. As she comes into breeding condition there develops in special pouches at the end of her abdomen a small supply of perfume, less than a ten-thousandth of a milligramme. When ready, she exposes the membranes lining the pouches to disseminate the perfume. The infinitesimal quantity of perfume is diffused through the atmosphere and it is sufficient if one molecule of it lodges on the antenna of a male eleven kilometres away to start him on his search for the female. At the most a few hundred molecules will suffice to give a strong response to carry him to the female to mate with her.

The small amount given out by any one female was shown by Adolf Butenandt, who had to take half a million virgin female silk moths to obtain twelve milligrammes of the pure perfume. When a glass rod dipped in a solution of the perfume in petroleum was held near the antenna of a male silk moth, the male began to vibrate his wings rapidly, although there could not have been more than a few molecules of perfume on the rod.

Whatever else we say about it these few statements underline the fact that the sense of smell works on incredibly small stimuli. The receptors themselves are also unbelievably small. In an insect antenna 0·2 mm in diameter are packed about 20,000 sense-cells and 40,000 nerve fibres and all but 5,000 of the nerve fibres are concerned with smell. Among the 35,000 nerve fibres there are specialists, which react to one or a few scents only, and generalizers, that react to a wide range of scents.

A male moth reacting to the perfume of a female will pick out the molecules of this one odour with one or more of its specialists and ignore the hosts of other odours present in the atmosphere through which it is flying, just as a tracker dog will select the odour from one person and follow this to the exclusion of all others.

What is not known, although there are several theories about it, is how a molecule hitting the smelling membrane sparks off the minute nerve impulses to the brain. Some scientists have suggested there is a chemical reaction between the end membrane of a receptor and the molecule touching it. The more currently accepted view is that a molecule of a particular shape must lodge in a receptor so shaped that it fits exactly into it, to set the current going. This is the lock-and-key theory, which is as reasonable as any, and as hard to prove or disprove as any other.

Another theory is that the characteristic peculiar to a smell molecule is its vibration. All atoms vibrate and the vibration of a molecule is the resultant of the vibrations of all the atoms in it. Thus every substance will have a unique pattern of vibrations and chemicals with similar vibrations will smell very much the same. It has been shown also that in mammals some of the cells lining the nose contain free vitamin A and protein-bound carotenoids. The second of these, so named because they are pigments first found in carrots, are probably the substances that receive energy from odour molecules. The molecules in rhodopsin, the visual purple of the eye, change shape when light falls on the eye, and it may be that there is a similar change in the chemically related carotenoids in the olfactory membrane which initiates the message to the brain.

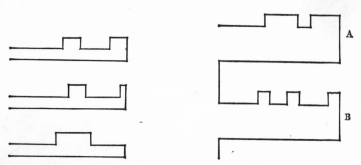

Graphic representation of the lock-and-key theory to explain the mechanism of smelling. Three 'keys' (left), representing molecules of three odorous substances, will fit 'lock' A but not 'lock' B. So although the keys have slightly different shapes they represent similar odours.

It may be that the molecules have different impacts on the olfactory membranes of different groups of animals, one theory holding for insects, another for fishes and so on.

For the time being the way in which the olfactory receptors are stimulated need provoke no more than an academic interest. More striking is the effect produced in the brain. Lord Adrian anaesthetized a hedgehog, inserted silver electrodes into its brain and held wads of cotton wool impregnated with odorous substances in front of the animal's nostrils. He recorded that with strongly smelling substances two-thirds of the surface of the brain were electrically activated, an effect comparable with a blinding flash in front of the eye.

The sense of smell is probably more universally distributed over the animal kingdom than any other of the senses apart from touch. It plays a major role in the search for and selection of food. In all but the lowest animals it plays a vital part in bringing the sexes together, notable exceptions among the higher animals being the birds and the primates (monkeys, apes and man). Again, with these exceptions, it plays a large part in the marking of territories and detecting the presence of enemies.

It has been suggested that alone among the senses the receptor cells for smell have been unchanged from the sea anemone to man. Throughout the animal kingdom they are simple cells with hair-like projections to receive the scent molecules. Any specializations involve only greater numbers crowded together, in the antennae, the nostrils or the skin, wherever the special organs of scent may be, and the addition of pigment.

It seems that there is a correlation between pigmentation and the sense of smell, which is highlighted by the strange case recorded in 1852 of a boy, the son of Negro parents in Kentucky, U.S.A. who was normal until the age of twelve. Then white patches appeared near the left eye and spread over his body until, ten years later, he was a 'white' except for his woolly hair. When the white patches first appeared he began to lose his sense of smell and in the end he lost it completely.

The linkage between the loss of pigment can also be illustrated by saying that in the higher animals the olfactory membrane varies from yellow to dark brown. In man it is reddish brown and in dogs it is dark brown, almost black. Dark-skinned men have more pigment in the eye than fair-skinned men, and also seem to have a more efficient sense of smell. Arabs of the Sahara are said to be able to smell a fire thirty miles away, and Negroes show a more acute sense of smell than Caucasians. The sense of smell in children is less than in adults and their olfactory membrane is far less pigmented. Similarly young animals are less pigmented in the nasal membrane than adults, and it is noticeable that dark clothes absorb odours more than light-coloured fabrics.

It can be argued that sight and hearing as well as smell suffer when pigment is lacking, an example being white domestic cats, that are usually deaf, but only if pure white. A single blotch of colour can alter this. With the sense of smell, also, the pigment is not in the sense-cells themselves. It need only be present in adjacent tissues. Tracker dogs, for example, have heavily pigmented areas around the muzzle and especially around the nostrils.

As with the taste-buds, the olfactory receptors soon suffer from fatigue. When we smell a flower the enjoyment of its perfume soon wanes, and if we persist in the smelling it goes altogether, but will soon revive. A tracker dog will pause every so often to clear its nostrils by breathing out through them, clearing the smelling membrane to bring it back to maximum efficiency.

The membrane is moistened with mucus, and although we commonly use the dog's nose as an indicator of health—when a dog's nose is dry it is unwell—the main purpose of the moisture may be as an accessory to smelling. This much we may deduce from the behaviour of the hedgehog, which probably has as acute a sense of smell as a dog. A tame hedgehog, kept in the house, will start to drip at the nose as a stranger enters the room, especially if picked up by that stranger. Whether this indicates disgust at the presence of an unusual odour, or is a means of clearing the olfactory membrane because of fatigue, is not known.

Over and above the size of the olfactory membrane, the moistness, the pigment, age and other factors that influence the efficiency of the smell organ, there must be individual variations. An example of such a variation between two human beings is furnished by the experience of a scientist and his wife standing on the platform of a large railway terminus in London. She, an ardent naturalist, was noted for her ability to smell the odour of a fox. As the two stood waiting for their train, in an atmosphere laden with a miscellany of odours, the wife sniffed the air and said: 'Fox!'

The husband told her he could not believe there was a fox within miles, but he nevertheless made it his business to inquire, and discovered that it was not unusual for foxes to scavenge around large railway stations for food from the restaurant cars.

Although the wife could unerringly pick up the odour of a fox she was unable to smell certain flowers which her husband could easily detect.

There is no information on how much individual variation there may be among wild animals of a given species. It is certain there is a wide individual variation among breeds of dogs, and also among individual dogs of each breed, judging solely from their performances.

This is a point too often ignored by those writing on animal senses. There was, for example, the famous experiment on whether a dog could succeed in distinguishing between identical twins. But first let us take one of the earliest experiments in this field. It was carried out by G. J. Romanes in 1885. Twelve men walked in single file, led by Romanes, each being careful to place his feet in the footsteps of the man in front. After a while the party split into two groups, each going its own way to a hiding-place. Romanes's dog was then released and she tracked her master to his hiding-place with little hesitation.

This and later experiments led to testing for identical twins. A party including the twins set off across a field then split into two, with one of the twins in each. The dog followed, having been allowed to sample the scent of one twin. It followed the trail of the wrong twin. Further tests showed that identical twins have very similar scents and a dog can only tell them apart if confronted by both scents at once.

It is always assumed that this must be true of all dogs. The likelihood is that it represents the average, which is remarkable enough, but the truth probably is that if enough dogs were tested it would be found that there are some dogs that would be able to track the correct twin, corresponding to the scent the dog had sampled, even if it had not been previously confronted by both at once.

There is another factor which can influence the acuity of a dog's sense of smell. W. Neuhaus fed some dogs on food to which a gramme of butyric acid had been added. Two hours later their sense of smell had deteriorated, but four or five days later they could smell anything containing butyric acid three times better than at the beginning of the experiment.

This could be important to a wild dog feeding on the carcase of a kill, which would contain butyric acid. It would gorge itself and not feed for several days, by which time its hunger would have returned and its sense of smell for its prey would have increased in efficiency. It would then be at its peak for tracking the prey animal, even to making use of trails tending to fade out with age.

While still on mammals, there is a curious reaction to odour discovered among mice which leads to a population control. A female laboratory mouse, recently mated, will fail to achieve pregnancy if she is subjected to the odour at close quarters of a male other than the one she mated with. Therefore when crowded together, as mice would be in a population explosion, most or all of the females fail to bear young.

In contrast to the keen sense of smell of most animals, birds give little indication in their behaviour of anything but a poor sense of smell; so poor, in fact, that it is usual to say they are without a sense of smell. This is generally true, although some sea-birds as well as ducks probably have at least a mediocre sense of smell. The fulmar, a North Atlantic petrel, has been tested and has been found to fly in from a fair distance when cooked meat, or the fat from it, is thrown into the sea. Fulmars used to gather around the whalers in the Arctic feeding on whale offal, and this started a phenomenal spread of the fulmar southwards to the coasts of the British Isles. As the whales died out the fulmars followed the fishing fleets for fish offal.

One bird that has been the subject of research in recent years is the New Zealand kiwi. It comes out at night to feed on earthworms, driving its long bill into the ground to find them. It is the only bird with nostrils at the tip of the bill, so it had always been assumed that the kiwi smells its prey, although this had not been proven. In 1968 Bernice Wenzel sank aluminium tubes in the ground in a kiwi reserve. Each tube was filled with earth and pieces of nylon sheet were stretched over the mouth of the tube and tied in position. Half the tubes had only earth in them, the others contained either earthworms or some other food. In the morning only the nylon over the tubes containing food had been punctured.

INTERNAL NOSTRIL

Diagrammatic section through the head of a snake showing the position of Jacobson's organ. A snake flickers its tongue, pushing it out then withdrawing it. When withdrawn the twin tips are pressed into two cavities in the roof of the mouth. These cavities together make up Jacobson's organ, an organ of smell.

Reptiles have a fair sense of smell, and snakes have a specialized organ in the roof of the mouth known as Jacobson's organ. This consists of two sensory pits, richly supplied with nerve endings, that are formed from the nasal cavities during the development of the embryo. A snake flicking its tongue out and in is something that has been known about for a long time. Formerly the tongue was thought to be poisonous, a kind of sting. Then it was suspected of being an organ of touch, which it may be partly. Now it is known to be used in the sense of smell.

The tongue is protruded and withdrawn through a small gap in the lips, in front, without opening the mouth. While protruded the forked tongue flickers, picking up odorous particles floating in the air, only sometimes touching solid objects. When the tongue is withdrawn the two tips of the tongue are inserted into the twin pits in the roof of the mouth and the odorous particles transferred to them.

As an example of how keen the sense of smell may be in other reptiles, it is worth recounting the gruesome story told by Karl P. Schmidt and Robert F. Inger in their *Living Reptiles of the World*. An elderly Indian in Indiana, U.S.A., had a reputation for his ability to recover the bodies of drowned persons. He kept a large snapping turtle which he would take to a lake where a fatality was suspected, and in a short while would locate the body. His method was to release the turtle from a boat after attaching a long wire to it. Allowing the turtle a little while to explore the water and pick up the scent of the corpse, the Indian would follow the line to where the turtle was about to feed on the body.

A first-class clue to the smelling abilities of the higher animals is in the proportions of the brain. In the front of the brain is a pair of olfactory lobes in which the information from the olfactory membranes is processed. In fishes these are relatively large. In sharks they are enormous, and sharks find their food mainly by scent. In birds, for the most part, these lobes are very small.

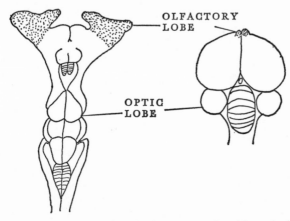

The proportions of certain parts of the brain are a rough guide to the importance of the senses. In the shark's brain (left) the olfactory lobes are large, the optic lobes are small and hidden. A shark hunts by smell, its eyes being of indifferent use. The bird's brain (right) shows feeble olfactory lobes and large optic lobes.

Sharks are not alone among fishes in hunting by smell. Eels also are scavengers and hunt in the murky depths of lakes and rivers, and usually at night. The moray eel does much the same, but one of its prey animals is the octopus which, according to popular belief, gives out a cloud of ink which acts as a smoke-screen under cover of which the octopus retreats. That is the popular idea; yet, if one takes an eye-dropper (or the old-fashioned fountain-pen filler) and squirts a quantity of ink into a large bowl of water there is a perceptible passage of time before the ink disperses sufficiently to make a protective cloud. Meanwhile there would be time enough for the moray to have seized the octopus.

The truth, as shown a few years ago, is that the ink contains a chemical which temporarily puts the moray's sense of smell out of action. The eel must catch the octopus unawares or lose its quarry.

There are two other ways in which the sense of smell plays a large part in the lives of fishes. One is familiar, the other was unsuspected until a few years ago. The familiar way is the use of smell in migrating fishes, the best-known example being the salmon which, hatched in the upper reaches of a river, goes down to the sea and after several years finds its way back to its natal stream to spawn.

For a long time this had baffled zoologists. Then in 1957 L. R. Donaldson and G. H. Allen took salmon spawn from a stream in the Rocky Mountains and put it in another stream several hundred miles away. The young salmon hatching from it went to the sea as usual, but instead of going back to the stream where the spawn was laid they returned to the stream in which they were hatched.

Five years later A. D. Hasler caught 300 salmon returning in two arms of the Issaquah River. He blocked the nostrils of half of these with cotton wool, took all to a point downstream of the fork and returned them to the river. Those with nostrils free had no hesitation in choosing the arm of the river from which they had been taken. The rest blundered about in the river below the fork, unable to follow any direction. There can be no question of whether it is the taste of the natal water or smell that guides the salmon. The nostrils of most fishes do not connect with the mouth. They are pits in the top of the head, near the front, usually two communicating pits to each nostril. Each pit is lined with an olfactory membrane puckered into ridges to present a large surface to receive the particles of odour.

The unexpected discovery was that injured fishes release into the water from their wounds odoriferous substances. When these reach the nostrils of their fellows they induce an alarm reaction. The school breaks up and the individual fishes scatter in all directions. This was first discovered in the European minnow, but a number of other fishes have been shown to react in the same way. There are, however, exceptions, especially among those species such as sharks that will swallow the dismembered remains of their own kind.

It is hardly surprising that smell should play so large a part in the lives of fishes. Tests on eels have shown, for example, that their sense of smell exceeds that of dogs. Even in human beings, with so weak a sense of smell, the perfume of a flower or the scent of pinewood can evoke a flood of vivid, if ill-defined, memories of childhood. So it is easy to see how the odour of the natal stream, carried downriver and dispersing into the sea, can guide a salmon.

The sense of smell in animals without backbones is, as in the backboned animals, intimately associated with taste, and in the lower forms the two are often impossible to separate. It is usual then to refer to a common chemical sense. In insects more particularly, however, a definite sense of smell can be identified, usually in the antennae, but sometimes there are olfactory receptors on the mouth parts as well.

It is relatively easy to demonstrate this. When a piece of strong-smelling cheese is brought near a cockroach, for example, the insect's antennae can be seen waving in the air and then directed towards the cheese, after which the cockroach, with its antennae still directed towards it, walks towards the cheese. If the antennae are cut off, or coated with a varnish, the cockroach shows no interest in the cheese. When there are accessory organs of smell on the mouth parts as well, cutting off the antennae only reduces the insect's sense of smell. Coating the mouth parts with varnish obliterates it completely.

Some of the earliest experiments on the sense of smell in insects were crude but convincing; indeed they were carried out almost by accident by moth collectors. A virgin female placed in a box, for collecting purposes, would attract numbers of males in a very short time. Even when the female was removed, the box with her odour still clinging to it would attract as many male moths as the female herself. It also happened at times that the collector would, in taking home his box, thereby remove a female to a district not normally inhabited by her species. Since males still continued to assemble around the box they must have flown from a long distance.

More refined experiments during the present century confirmed the results of these almost accidental experiments and carried them further. Then it was found that not only does the female give off a perfume to attract the male, but that in many species the male moth, on reaching the female, gives off a perfume that overpowers her—a kind of sedative—making her receptive to mating. It also seems to act as a repellent to other males arriving on the scene.

The mating of insects is entirely unromantic. A few molecules landing on the antennae of a male moth automatically sets his wings vibrating. A few more molecules and he takes to the air, flying into the wind carrying the molecules. If he overshoots his target, so that no more molecules are bombarding his antennae, he lands, reconnoitres with his antennae, even crawling on the ground meanwhile, until he can once more locate the female and fly to her.

The antennae also act as direction-finders. If more molecules are reaching the right-hand antennae than the left the moth alters course slightly to the right, until both antennae are equally stimulated. Experimenters have crossed the antennae of insects and fastened them in that position. Insects so treated can never reach their target—they are continually turning away from the stream of odorous particles, utterly confused.

There are, however, several instances in which males released 1·6 km away reached the female ten minutes later. They must, therefore, have flown at not less than 10 km an hour, which is just over twice the walking pace of a man. Therefore they could not have spent much time in searching flights. For the rest, males have been known to find their way to a female from distances of 5 km, even 11 or 20 km, but in these cases it is not certain that they flew direct. It is suspected that they make reconnaissance flights until they have picked up the scent stream. But since it is fairly certain that the male can detect the female at a distance of 1·6 km it looks as if the emperor moth has at least as keen a sense of smell as an elephant, which is said to be able to pick up odours 1·6 km away.

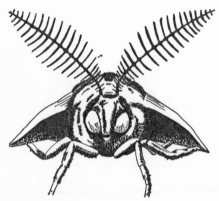

Looking into the face of a male moth with the feathered antennae, organs of smell, raised above the eyes. A tiny particle of perfume from a female moth releases millions of molecules into the air. Although these become highly dispersed over a distance, a few only falling on a minimal number of the tens of thousands of receptor cells scattered over his antennae are needed to stimulate the male to home on the female.

Just as the smelling-membrane of a dog or an elephant is laid over much-folded bones in the nose to increase the surface offered to the scent particles, so the feathered antennae of a moth also offer a very large surface. The result is that a dog, elephant or moth can detect scents which are odourless to our noses. We, for example, cannot detect the scent given off by a female moth. We know it is there because it can be extracted in benzene, and this extract can be used to call the male moths in as certainly as if the female were there.

Insects share with dogs and with other animals having a keen sense of smell the ability to detect a scent even when it is masked by a more powerful odour. This was first shown to be so by Lord Lubbock, who years ago carried out experiments with ants. We know that ants find their way back to their nests by following scent trails. All the ants in a nest carry the same scent, so that a 'foreigner' can be easily detected and driven out. In their foraging expeditions ants follow well-worn paths. We see them passing and repassing along these trails, and if we smudge across the trail with a finger the ants will show signs of being lost when they come to the smudge.

Lord Lubbock took ants from two different nests and marked them with different colours so that he could see which ants came from which nest. He put them on a table and surrounded this with a moat containing water. Then he gave the ants alcohol, which they drank, so that they not only made themselves drunk and lay still as if dead, but each ant smelt, to the human nose, strongly of alcohol. A bridge was placed across the moat, near to one of the nests, so that only ants from that one nest crossed the moat. As soon as they reached the table and started to explore it they found the drunken ants. Those that came from their own nest they picked up and carried back into the nest. The others they drowned in the moat. This could only mean that they could detect the ants' own scent in spite of the alcohol.

Tests carried out some years later showed that blindfolded ants could find their way back to the nest easily. Yet when their antennae were coated with paste or glue, inhibiting their sense of smell, they failed to find their way back.

Another insect having a remarkable sense of smell is a small round black beetle which feeds on truffles. There is also a small fly that lays its eggs in them. Truffles are fungi which grow entirely underground, at anything down to 30 cm below the surface. Some people regard them as a delicacy, and to save themselves the labour of hunting for them use an animal to nose them out. A number of wild animals search for them of their own accord to eat them. These include the wild boar, wild cat, wolf, bear, deer, goat, badger, rabbit, squirrel and fieldmouse. In some countries dogs are trained to smell out the truffles. Pigs have also been used, and so have goats in Sardinia. Earth is a deodorant, that is, it tends to kill smells, which is one of the reasons why we bury anything that is evil smelling. It is the more surprising therefore that any animal should smell a truffle buried a foot deep in the earth. Only one human has been known to be able to smell out truffles. It is even more astonishing that goats and pigs should be better at it than dogs, which have to be trained and then often fail to find the truffles if their owners do not guide them to some extent.

The beetle and the fly can detect the truffles from a distance. From how great a distance we do not know, but a pig can smell the truffle in the earth from a distance of 50 m if the wind is right. At all events the insects can find the spot and then bore down through the earth, straight to the truffle and without ever making a mistake.

These are only a few of the more outstanding examples of how insects use their sense of smell. There are plenty of others, less spectacular, that go on all around us. The small wasps known as ichneumon flies lay their eggs in the bodies of large caterpillars. The eggs hatch and the young ichneumons feed on the fat inside the body of the caterpillar which, because no vital organ is touched, is able to keep going until the time for pupation, when it dies. Meanwhile the ichneumon larvae have been feeding and growing, and are themselves able to pupate when their host, the caterpillar, dies.

Clearly it would be uneconomical for a female ichneumon to lay her eggs in a caterpillar in which another ichneumon had already laid her eggs. And she never does so, for the simple reason that she can smell if another ichneumon has already landed on the caterpillar.

Bees use scent and the sense of smell not only to find nectar and pollen but in the household activities within the hive. When one bee meets another in the hive it may regurgitate a drop of food which the other takes from its mouth. In this way all members of the hive have the same odour, and it differs from the odour of bees from other hives. A bee going into a strange hive may pass undetected for a while, but it risks being recognized as a stranger and of being mauled or hustled out of the hive. Should several stranger bees go into a hive they are more likely to be detected. The whole hive then becomes alerted, and when this happens some of the bees, usually the younger workers, take up positions near the entrance to the hive. They are known as guard bees and they examine every bee approaching the entrance with their antennae. Any of their fellows are allowed to pass, a stranger is turned away, and provided it goes quietly it may suffer no harm.

Sometimes a guard bee may not be sure, on first examination, whether the newcomer is a stranger or not. It will then follow the newcomer into the hive, all the time examining it with the antennae.

Bees also use odour outside the hive. If one of them has found a good supply of nectar it will give off a scent trail which other bees pick up and are guided to the source of nectar. Such scent trails are more attractive to members of the same hive than to bees belonging to another hive.

Sometimes bees get lost. When a lost bee finally reaches the hive it stops at the entrance, raises its body, gives off a scent and fans it with its wings, dispersing it into the air. The trail guides the other lost bees to the hive.

Much is known about how bees use odours and about their sense of smell because they produce honey, a marketable product; so bees have been closely studied. For example, the workers recognize the queen by smell, and it is by smell that the hive keeps together as an organized society. When the queen is no longer with them the worker bees notice the absence of the queen-smell and become agitated.

The insects we have been considering are bees, ants, butterflies and beetles. These are all higher insects. There are the less advanced insects, usually called primitive, such as cockroaches, and the silver-fish we find in the bread-bin. The ancestors of these were on the earth 250 million years ago. This was long before the flowering plants appeared. These early insect ancestors did not have the same need of a sense of smell, certainly not for gathering nectar, and their descendants do not seem to have improved on it. It is only the insects that came later, when flowering plants had come into being, that seem to have an acute sense of smell.

Chapter 11

All manner of eyes

There are almost as many different kinds of eyes as there are species in the animal kingdom, provided we define as eyes any sense receptor sensitive to light. We can divide them into four types: the vertebrate eye, the compound eye, the simple eye and the light sensitive skin. Within each of these four groups are infinite variations, for no two species have precisely the same structure of eye. The differences may only be minor but they are there.

It is important to have this assessment firmly in mind as we approach our study of the sense of sight. We have to discard any previously held ideas that because the eyes of two species look alike the two kinds of animals see alike or use their eyes for the same purposes or for the same ends.

A few broad comparisons between familiar animals can be our starting point for a venture into a highly complex field of study. The lion, so far as we can tell, sees much as we do, able to distinguish detail at about 1·6 km distant, but it has better night vision. A rhinoceros sees objects as blurred as we do with our peripheral vision, which is why it is dangerous. Relying on its sense of smell, at first alarm it turns and charges upwind, in the direction from which our scent is reaching it. An elephant is much the same.

A horse, which has the largest eye of any land animal—but not the largest in proportion to its size—has acute vision, but cannot focus as well as we can. Arabian horses are said to be able to recognize their master from other men similarly dressed at a half-kilometre distance. Horses have slightly less efficient binocular vision, but have the advantage of all-round vision, able to see in front, to the sides, and as well to the rear as to the front. Indeed a horse can see straight forward and straight backward at the same time without moving its head, and is very sensitive to moving objects all round its field of vision.

Rats and mice, despite their relatively large and seemingly bright eyes, are very short-sighted. It is possible to bring one's face within a few inches of one of them and produce no reaction, provided this is done slowly and noiselessly. The slightest sound will, however, have an immediate effect. The myopia of rodents is no great disadvantage since they are active mainly at night and by day operate mainly in dim light, only exceptionally coming out into full light.

Squirrels have a fixed stare, so that the expression on the face entirely lacks animation. But they have no need to move the eyes as these give all-round vision, more completely than in a horse.

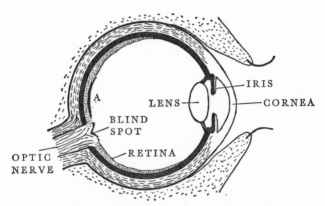

Cross-section through the human eye as a typical representative of the mammalian eye. Basically the eye is constructed on the same principles as a camera, but the working of the sense of sight as a whole, including the processing by the optic nerve and the brain, make this a crude comparison. A = area of maximum visual acuity.

The most acute vision is among birds of prey. Tests have shown that falcons can distinguish details which a man can only pick out using binoculars that magnify eight times. What this means in practice can be gauged from what we can more readily see in small songbirds, with less acute vision than the birds of prey. For example, a small songbird we are watching may suddenly crouch and cock its head in a typical 'hawk alarm' reaction. We look around and finally see a dot in the sky which might be any kind of bird, or even not a bird at all. Our small songbird has not only seen it before we did, it has also recognized it as a hawk, as we do when it flies nearer. This was long ago recognized by falconers, whose trained birds might fly out of sight. They carried a caged shrike, and by watching the way the crouching shrike was cocking its head the falconer could direct his gaze to the sky and so pick out the dot high overhead that represented his falcon.

We can only assess the sight of animals by comparison with our own. It is the only standard we have outside the laboratory. Yet those who study the human eye agree it is not the efficient organ we tend to believe it is. Not only have birds keener sight than we have, most insects can distinguish rapidly moving objects far better than we can. Indeed experts on human vision assure us that we only see as correctly as we do because our imagination compensates for our deficiencies in seeing—a sobering thought when so much scientific research depends on the eyes of the researcher! An example of how the imagination assists the vision is seen in cartoons, when a few lines drawn by the artist suggest to us a well-known person.

To test this, A. Hajos of Innsbruck University and his students wore spectacles with distorting lens for days on end, during which time they first saw straight lines as curved, sharp outlines fringed with colour, objects displaced and strange movements as they moved their heads. After about a week, however, they began to see things normally. Their imaginations were correcting the distortions. And apparently this is happening with us all the time.

One of the main reasons why the eyes of vertebrates differ from one species to another is that the proportions of rods and cones in the retina varies widely. Rods are elongated rod-shaped cells in the retina, cones are shorter and plumper, cone-shaped in their outer half. Rods give no colour vision in any light, and are especially a feature of the eyes of nocturnal animals. Our retina is made up of these two kinds of cells, the cones being packed mainly in a small central area, the fovea centralis. We see only a small area of our visual field sharply, the part that falls on the fovea. All around this is indistinct, making up our peripheral vision.

When we say we see an image sharply, even this is an illusion. The eyeball is never compeletly still. If it were we should see an image criss-crossed with dark lines, like the picture on a television screen looked at close to, because the 283 units making up the human fovea do not form a continuous sensitive sheet but are each separate. The eyeball is continuously on the move, in a microscopic tremor, so that an image looks perfect. It is a similar illusion to that of a ciné film, in which thirty-two separate frames are moving across the screen per second yet the picture looks like a steady image.

It is by the examination of the rods and cones that a fair estimate can be made how far an animal enjoys colour vision. We know that apes and monkeys, birds, most reptiles and fishes, and many insects have colour vision, although they do not necessarily see the same bands of the spectrum as we do. Of the more familiar animals, about which it has so often been said that they see the world as shades of grey, dogs and cats are now known to have a faint colour vision, while horses, sheep, pigs and squirrels can see a few colours. Giraffes can see some colours, but confuse green, orange and yellow.

The retina is made up of rods and cones and millions of nerve cells. In the human eye the light from an image strikes 130 million visual nerve cells. The light is absorbed by the visual pigment in the retina

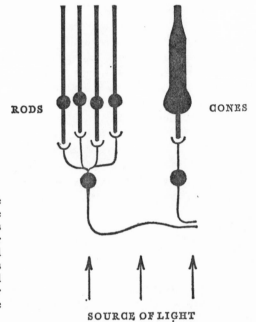

RODS

CONES

The retina of the eye is made up entirely of rods in some species and of rods and cones in others. Cones enable colour vision and each cone is served by a single nerve fibre. Rods are especially sensitive to small movements but give no colour vision. Four rods are here served by one nerve fibre.

SOURCE OF LIGHT

and converted into electrical energy. This varies with the quantity of light entering the eye. But the retina does more than convert light into electrical activity for transmission along the million nerve fibres of the optic nerve to the brain. It is not simply a matter of the stronger the light falling on the eye the stronger—that is, the more frequent—the impulses reaching the brain.

A good deal of processing of information goes on in the various layers of the retina itself. There are three main layers of nerve cells arranged perpendicularly to the surface of the retina and two horizontal layers alternating with them, all connected in a highly complex network system. Each cell in the horizontal layers sends out branching fibres which connect with similar branching fibres from neighbouring cells. Where two branches meet a chemical reaction can take place between them, transferring energy from one cell to another. Some branches in each cell are excitatory, others are inhibitory. As in a discussion, some people advocate action while others are for doing nothing, in the end reaching a decision intermediate between the two, so the excitatory and inhibitory cells argue and decide which information shall go forward and which shall be delayed.

At this microscopic level it is difficult to be more precise or even to take the matter much further without bursting into language incomprehensible to all but the specialist. A simple example will, however, help. When watching a moving target the human eye must lead the target, just as a hunter aims his rifle just ahead of a flying bird or a running hare. A message to the brain would take too long. Thirty milliseconds are required for the reaction of the retinal cells, five milliseconds for the message to reach the brain and 100 milliseconds for the brain to sort out the information to produce the image, by which time the position of the object in space will have altered. The retina, accordingly, sorts out this information itself.

Another illusion to be set aside is that all animal eyes, or even all vertebrate eyes, provide their owners with photographic images. A frog has a more efficient retina than that of the human eye, yet its vision is strictly limited. It sees only a uniform dark background and only four things register on it: these are straight edges, moving forms that are convex in front, changes of contrast and a rapid darkening of the background. The moving convex forms represent the usual shape of the front end of an insect and spell food. But a frog does not appreciate movement in every direction, only movement towards itself, that is, within reach of its tongue which can be shot out to catch insects. The advantage of appreciating only changes in contrast is that the frog is not bemused by such things as waving grass. The appreciation of a rapid darkening of the background helps when, for example, a heron comes flying in or moves towards the frog.

We can see now why the toad mentioned in Chapter 4 could not tell a small grass snake from an earthworm by looking at it.

A frog's eye also reacts to colour, but to a limited extent. In moments of alarm a frog is attracted to blue, which usually represents water, but a frog will equally jump onto a sheet of blue paper laid down before it. Simultaneously with blue becoming attractive, green becomes repellent, making the frog move away from vegetation to the blue of water.

The retinas of the pigeon and the rabbit, as well as that of the frog, are also more highly organized than those of monkeys and man. This is explained by the fact that more processing of information takes place in their retinas, whereas in monkeys and men the information from their less highly organized retinas is to a greater extent passed on to the brain for processing. To understand why this is we need to know how the eye of a vertebrate comes into being.

In the early stages of the embryo the spinal cord takes shape as a hollow tube running the length of the embryo body. The portion in front begins to grow more rapidly than the rest of the spinal cord. It swells and so lays the foundations of the future brain. On either side of it grows out a stalked cup, almost the shape of a brandy glass. Meanwhile from the skin of the embryo a disc-shaped piece of tissue migrates inwards to fit into the mouth of the 'brandy glass' to form the lens. The retina of the eye is therefore a part of the brain, and its structure is very similar to that of the cortex of the brain. So in the frog, pigeon and rabbit, some of the 'thinking' is done in this outlier of the brain we call the retina, and in monkeys and men, with their larger, more highly organized brains, the retina need not be as highly organized as in a frog, pigeon or rabbit because more work can be passed on to the brain to deal with.

We tend to speak, in talking about the eyes of animals, as if we had complete knowledge of all of them. There are over a million species of animals and we do not have complete knowledge of the eyes or the vision of any one of them. Moreover the number that have been studied in any detail amounts to no more than scores. The frog, pigeon and rabbit are familiar laboratory animals, as every biology student knows, so they have received attention. Monkeys and men are used in the more advanced studies.

The eyes of birds, also, have been fairly well studied, at least in their gross structure, so we can say with confidence that the highest development of the eye is in birds; and it is equalled in some lizards. In birds there are three types of eye: flat, globose and tubular. The first may be called the normal eye, because it is found in the majority of birds. The second is found in birds of prey, such as eagles. The third is found in owls, the nocturnal birds of prey.

An unusual feature of the eye of all birds is the pecten, which is like a comb attached to the back of the eye and lying freely in the cavity of the eye. It is usually pleated and richly served with blood vessels. It is smallest in owls, largest in eagles and hawks, and probably serves only to nourish the retina, which contains no blood vessels. Nevertheless a bird's retina is thick with numerous interconnections, and is superior in this to the human retina.

Eagles and hawks, as well as owls, have very large eyes. In some species they are as big as the head can accommodate, the two eyeballs almost touching except for a thin body septum between them, although from the outside they look no larger than usual. There is, therefore, little room for the muscles that move the eyeball, and in hawks only horizontal movement is possible. In the case of owls, which have tubular eyes, no movement at all is possible because the eye so completely fills the orbit, so the bird must turn its head, using its flexible neck, and it can do this through 180° either way.

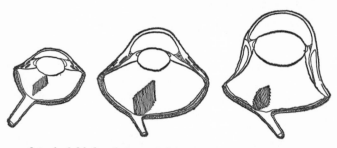

The eyes of typical birds: (left to right) a swan, eagle and owl; the eyebal being seen here is transverse section, to show differing shapes. In addition to the cornea, lens and retina a prominent feature of the eyes of birds is the pecten, richly supplied with blood vessels, probably for nourishing the organ as a whole.

The globose shape of the eye of eagles and hawks gives acute vision. The lens in it is flattened and, because of the shape of the eye, is situated at a greater distance than usual from the retina, giving a larger image on the retina—a sort of telephoto lens. There are more cones than rods over the whole retina and there is a central area, the fovea, of tightly packed cones, each with its own fibre running into the optic nerve. This means each cone can send its independent message to the brain, making for an appreciation of fine detail.

Birds that catch insects on the wing share the globose eye with the diurnal birds of prey, and so do the crow family, as well as hummingbirds. A practical demonstration of this by a member of the crow family was given by a tame jay that flew over to take an insect 2 m away. The insect was so small that it was difficult to see it with the human eye when the jay returned holding it in the tip of its beak.

Some birds, such as swallows and swifts, have a second fovea in each eye which gives them binocular vision. When pursuing small insects on the wing they can keep their eyes focused on their quarry and judge distance accurately while moving at high speeds. On one occasion a swift was seen to overtake a butterfly, which fluttered slowly to the ground as the bird sped on. But the butterfly was without head and body as it lay on the ground. The swift had so accurately snapped up its body, and with so little disturbance, although travelling so fast, that the wings had come to the ground together as if still joined by the body.

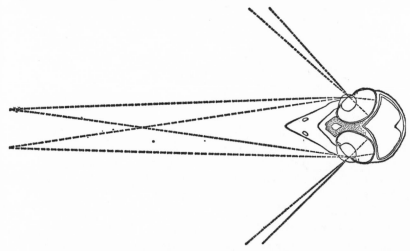

A combination diagram of the fields of intense vision in birds (the skull and beak being shown in section). With a single fovea the field of maximum vision is shown by the ray (dotted lines) to either side. In birds such as swallows, with a second fovea, binocular vision is indicated by the two rays (dotted) overlapping in front of the beak.

Such exploits require full daylight, so most diurnal birds go to roost fairly early in the evening. Yet there are wide differences in this respect. Some continue active almost until nightfall. Swifts continue hunting well after sunset, often in the company of noctule bats, and a male blackbird will continue singing until it is almost dark and has been known to mob an owl single-handed when the human eye could only make out the two birds when they were silhouetted against the sky.

Anyone working in the garden in the twilight can still see weeds which, were he to come from a lighted room, would be invisible to him unless he accustomed his eyes to the dim light for ten minutes. A pigeon would take an hour to adapt to the poor illumination. A barn-yard cock, on the other hand, whose sight is only one-tenth that of man in full daylight, will be active and crowing loudly when there is only the grey light preceding the dawn and when most other birds have hardly begun to stir.

Those birds best able to see at night are, however, the owls, with their tubular eyes, the third type of eye. Their secret is that their eyes are so constructed that they admit as much light as possible. The eye itself is large and so are the cornea and the lens, and there is an extra muscle for altering the shape of the cornea. Their binocular vision also helps in judging distances.

Aquatic birds face a peculiar difficulty, the need to see under water as well as in air. When under water the focusing effect of the cornea is lost, so they need to have a greater power of focusing with the lens. In such birds as cormorants, divers, auks and diving ducks, the lens is soft and can be squeezed into a pear shape, giving it increased power, and the cormorant's ability to alter the focus of the lens is five times greater than ours. Penguins, however, lack such an ability and are adapted to see well under water but are short-sighted in air. Terns dive and strike blindly at a fish, and so does the gannet. The kingfisher can see as well under water as in air, but the reason for this is not known.

Whereas land animals, including those that spend much time in water, accommodate the eyes to vision at varying distances by altering the shape of the lens, fishes achieve the same end by changing its position. A special muscle can move the lens nearer to or farther from the retina. Otherwise the eyes of fishes work much like our own, except that fishes lack binocular vision. There are, however, modifications largely unknown elsewhere among vertebrates. The four-eyed fish of Central and South America has eyes that project well above the top of the head, each being divided into halves by a dark horizontal band. The structure of the top half differs from that of the lower half and is used for vision in air, the lower half being for under-water vision. Four-eyed fishes swim in shoals just under the surface with the upper halves only of their eyes above the surface, so they can see insects skimming the surface or flying over it, while watching for anything edible in the water. The whirligig beetle, among insects, has similar eyes for the same purposes.

Some oceanic fishes have telescopic eyes, cylindrical and pro-truding, with a large spherical lens covered with a rounded cornea. In some species these are directed forwards, in others upwards. Sometimes there is a small accessory retina on the side of the tube just below the lens for focusing distant objects while the main retina is in focus for near objects. Deep-sea fishes living in the twilight zone, where daylight is petering out, tend to have very large lenses, wide

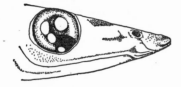 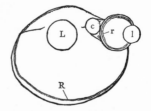

There is a second fish, besides that of Central and South America, known as the four-eyed fish. It is a deep-sea fish (head shown left, eye right). The deep-sea four-eyed fish lives at depths of 300 to 3,000 feet, in the twilight zone. The main eye has a subsidiary eye, presumably to increase acuity and also to give all-round vision.
L = lens, R = retina of main eye, l and r = corresponding structures of subsidiary eye, c = corneal body which probably bends light into main eye.

pupils and highly sensitive retinas of rods only. Their eyes are, in fact, very like owls' eyes.

Another way of making use of small amounts of light, as at night, is by use of the tapetum, a layer of silvery crystals behind the retina that acts as a reflector and is the cause of an animal's eyes shining in the dark. In a normal eye much of the light which enters passes through the retina between the rods or cones and is absorbed in the tissue behind it. The tapetum reflects such light back, so there is a second chance for it to strike the receptor cells in the retina. A cat's eyes, for example, use 50 per cent more of the available light than our eyes, so a cat can see six times better than we can in the dark, but the disadvantage of a tapetum is that as the light crosses the retina twice the image is blurred.

So far we have considered mainly mammals, birds and fishes. Starting at the lower levels of animal life we can trace a possible evolution of the eye. In its simplest form, in the single-celled animals (Protozoa) it is no more than a pigment spot sensitive to light. With it the animal is attracted to light. The next step is for a simple lens to overlie the pigment spot, concentrating the light on the pigment. The lower animals have at most these beginnings of an eye.

In earthworms, so sensitive to the sudden flashing of a white light, the light receptors are scattered over the body. These have no lens, retina or any other accessory structures, and the worm uses them only for distinguishing between light and darkness or assessing the brightness of a light. A shadow falling on an earthworm projecting from its burrow makes it draw back. This is its only defence against birds, and not a very effective one. A sea urchin in the Caribbean is known to have similar light receptors in its skin. It has long slender spines, and, when a shadow falls on it, the spines on their ball-and-socket joints with the body move until their points are directed towards the source of the shadow—and therefore towards a possible attacker.

Slightly higher in the evolutionary scale, organs of vision become elaborated to form simple eyes or ocelli. In some animals, such as molluscs, there may be several such ocelli scattered over the body. The scallop is outstanding in having a row of jewel-like ocelli around the edge of its body and visible when its shell gapes. Many insects have ocelli in addition to their compound eyes, which are described below. We know these are used by bees as a light meter. A foraging bee should not leave the hive too early in the morning before there is enough light for it to see the flowers, nor should it set out on a nectar-collecting expedition so late at the end of the day that it cannot return before dark. Its ocelli give it the appropriate information.

A caterpillar has no compound eyes like the adult butterfly or moth, only a row of six ocelli on each side of its head. Each ocellus has only a single retinal rod below the lens. A caterpillar feeding on the foliage of trees needs to be able to recognize a tree. It scans with its ocelli, and by moving its head in different directions can estimate the shape of a dark object. A caterpillar may make mistakes, as when it crawls up a man's leg, but usually it can make out the thickest and tallest tree within its own walking distance. Moreover it can do this even when eleven of its twelve eyes have been covered with black paint.

Others of the higher animals without backbones, notably insects, have compound eyes, each composed of a number of units, or ommatidia, fundamentally similar to a simple eye but more elaborate and crowded together to form a retina. Octopuses, cuttlefish and squid are exceptional in having an eye more like our own in appearance but like the eye of a frog in performance.

A compound eye is made up of a number of units, or ommatidia, each in effect a complete eye typically separated from its neighbours by an opaque layer of pigment. Each ommatidium has a cornea, formed from a clear section of the insect's cuticle, and a lens which focuses light on the seven to eight cells of the retinula (or small retina), which is connected by nerves to the brain. Each of the retinula cells has a rod-like, light-conducting rhabdomere running down its inner face.

The surface of an insect's compound eye, such as that of a dragon-fly with 28,000 ommatidia in each eye, looks like the surface of a honeycomb. Some of the earliest attempts to solve the question of how the eye worked included peeling the cuticle with its numerous facets and taking a photograph through it. The image of the object photographed was repeated in every facet. Later it was assumed that the insect saw things as we should through a diamond-paned leaded window, if we could only see light or darkness through each pane, and that the eye built up a mosaic of dots of varying intensity depending on the amount of light falling on each of the ommatidia.

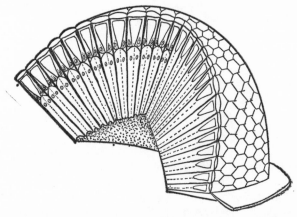

A typical compound eye, shown partly in section, made up of numerous ommatidia. The corneal lenses of the ommatidia are seen as a 'honeycomb' on the surface. Each ommatidium has a corneal lens at its outer surface, beneath this a crystalline cone and below this, running down the centre (dotted line), a retinal rod leading to a nerve fibre that connects with the brain.

This seemed to fit in with the observed sensitivity of insects to movements. A dragonfly with its high number of ommatidia can distinguish movement at a distance of 13 m, whereas worker ants with only a few appear to be oblivious of movements near at hand. Using the analogy of the diamond-paned window, it was like, so the theory supposed, the movement of a person going slowly past the window. With only a few large panes little movement would be seen, but with a large window made up of many small panes a moving person some distance from the window would cause a change in the brightness in successive panes and be readily detectable.

This theory, difficult to understand, broke down when tests were made using micro-electrodes that recorded the nerve impulses coming from a single ommatidium. Each ommatidium receives light over an arc ten times wider than had previously been supposed, which means that the compound eye sees more than was thought possible. But although the accepted theory of how the compound eye works has been proved untenable, no new theory can yet be put forward to replace it, except that it is now realized that the mechanism is much more complicated than was thought and involves complex nervous pathways as in the vertebrate retina.

What we can ourselves see of the behaviour of some insects supports the findings of the micro-electrodes. Hunting wasps are small insects that sting and paralyse other insects to store them in nests for their larvae to feed on. Each species shows an instinctive preference for one kind of prey, perhaps a species of spider, beetle, fly or bee. It might be thought that they do this by recognizing gross features, except for the behaviour of one hunting wasp that captures hoverflies. These have bodies striped yellow and black like wasps. It has always been said that hoverflies benefit from looking like wasps. People mistake them, but a hunting wasp will kill hoverflies and ignore wasps. Unless it is using some other sense in identifying hoverflies, its vision must be far better than anyone had supposed. This seems confirmed by laboratory tests.

Insects also see colours. K. von Frisch, famous for his discoveries on the language of bees, showed also how bees responded to colour. He trained them to feed on sugar water in bowls placed on blue paper. Once they were used to this he merely put blue paper down. The bees still came to it. If pieces of grey paper of varying shades were put around the blue, the bees still chose the blue.

By these training experiments von Frisch showed that bees could distinguish six colours: ultra-violet, bluish green, violet, bee's purple, yellow and blue. Their colour range covers another part of the spectrum from ours. Bees cannot see red, we cannot see ultra-violet. A poppy is red to us, but it also radiates ultra-violet, which we cannot see but a bee can, so it appears purplish to a bee. Other flowers appear black to a bee, but they have ultra-violet lines or other marks on their petals which guide a bee to the nectaries. These are known as honeyguides.

Flowers that look yellow to us look different to a bee according to how much ultra-violet they radiate. Mustard, rape and charlock look yellow to us; they look yellow, purple and crimson respectively to a bee. The common daisy radiates ultra-violet only at the tips of the petals, forming a halo as seen by a bee.

A few insects, the tortoiseshell butterfly being one, can see red. They feed especially at red flowers which radiate no ultra-violet. A

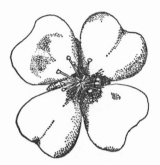 

The eye of a bee covers a different part of the spectrum from ours, so bees see flowers in different colours from us. (Left) A flower of Potentilla as we see it (allowing for the absence of colour) and (right) as a bee sees it. The pattern of lines and dark areas visible to the bee guides it to the nectaries. A Potentilla flower photographed using ultra-violet light gives the same effect.

wasp is unable to distinguish between black and red, but a firefly will respond to light between green and deep red.

Much of the research on the colour vision of insects is based on training experiments such as were first used by von Frisch. Sometimes these are useless. When a female cabbage white butterfly is about to lay her eggs she drums with her forefeet on the surface of a leaf. When presented with differently coloured paper she will drum on green or bluish green, the colours of leaves, but will make feeding movements of the tongue on red, yellow, blue and violet, the colours of the flowers she feeds on. Experiments with sugared water alone would have made it appear that the cabbage white butterfly was unable to recognize green.

F. E. Lutz had two notices painted in white letters on a black background: 'Bees may feed here' and 'No bees allowed here'. The bees appeared to be able to read and obey these notices, but Lutz had painted the first with process white, which radiates ultra-violet light. The second was painted with Chinese white, which does not radiate ultra-violet and so was invisible to the bees.

Both male and female luna moths look green to our eyes and are hidden from their enemies when resting on leaves. However, since the moths can see ultra-violet light which their bodies radiate, each sex is vividly obvious to the other on a green background. According to Lorus J. and Margery Milne the female looks blonde to the male and the male is brunette to the female.

Chapter 12

Celestial navigation

Beekeepers have long known that when one bee finds a source of nectar it is not long before it tells the other worker bees in the hive where it is. In 1946 it was established that bees do indeed talk to one another about where nectar and pollen are to be found.

In that year Karl von Frisch, who had already achieved fame for his discoveries about bees' colour vision, published his findings on bees' language. He had already noted several years before that a foraging bee on returning to the hive danced on the comb in one of two ways in what von Frisch called the round dance and the tail-wagging dance. He had the idea that the round dance told other bees coming into contact with the dancing bee that it had found a source of nectar, while the tail-wagging dance told them where to look for pollen.

Now he had found that the dances meant much more than this. The round dance indicated that the bee had found nectar or pollen within 50 m of the hive and the tail-wagging dance meant it had found them 100 m or more away. The distances in between were indicated by a gradual change-over from one kind of dance to the other.

In a round dance the bee turns round in circles on the same spot, first in one direction, then in the other. In the tail-wagging dance the bee runs in a figure-of-eight, making first a half-circle to the right then back to the starting point, to describe a similar half-circle to the left. All the time it is doing this, repeating the figure-of-eight, it is slowly wagging its abdomen from side to side.

Von Frisch had come upon this discovery about the distance-indicator while watching bees feeding at saucers of sugared water. Now he started to move the saucers farther and farther away, until they were 1·35 km from the hive. To his surprise and joy he noticed that the farther the bee had to travel back to the hive the more slowly it waggled its abdomen when it arrived there. From this he deduced that the bees were able to give their fellow foragers a fairly exact idea of the distance between the hive and a particular source of food by the number of waggles in the dance.

Then came an even greater surprise. The returning bees were also telling their fellow foragers the direction in which to go. The important part of the dance for this is the straight run along the middle of the figure of eight. If a bee, while dancing on a vertical surface, moves straight upwards to make the waist of the figure of eight, it is saying that the nectar or pollen is in the direction of the

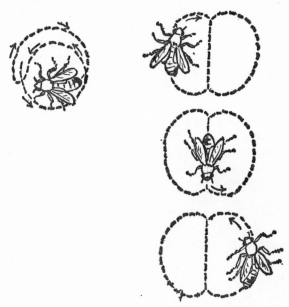

The discovery of the language of bees marked the start of a breakthrough into the vast field of celestial navigation. (Left) The round dance and (right) the tail-wagging dance. In an observation hive the bee performing the dance is surrounded and jostled by the other workers striving to get the message.

sun. If it goes straight downwards, the direction is opposite to that in which the sun lies. When its movement makes an angle to the right of the vertical then the other bees must seek food at a corresponding angle to the right of the position of the sun, and so on. At all times the bee alters the angle it makes to the vertical to correspond with the movement of the sun overhead. On one occasion, for example, one of von Frisch's students was keeping a dancing bee under observation. Its dance went on for eighty-four minutes, during which time the main axis of the dance gradually shifted 33°. During the same time the sun's azimuth had swung 34°.

The way in which the other bees get the message is by jostling around the dancing bee. Their bodies keep touching its body, and they also keep on touching it with their antennae.

In fact the dancing bee was using not so much the sun as the polarized light from the sky, that is the light-waves travelling in one plane in contrast to ordinary light-waves that go out in all directions. It could do this even with an overcast sky, with no sun visible, so long as there was even a small patch of blue showing through. Only when the sky was completely overcast was it unable to perform.

Early in his experiments von Frisch wanted to see what the bees would do on a horizontal instead of a vertical surface. He found they performed the same dance, but now the direction indicated by the dance corresponded exactly to that in which the food supply lay. Even more astonishing, if a bee were on a vertical comb and this was slowly moved to the horizontal, the bee gradually passed from one method of giving its information to the other. There was never any doubt about the meaning of the dance at any given moment, even to von Frisch, let alone the other bees.

Then came something even more astounding than the dance itself. After a reconnoitring flight which has taken it in all directions, so that by ordinary standards the bee ought to be hopelessly lost, it can turn and fly directly back to the hive. Its brain, like a computer, has taken note of all the twists and turns in relation to the sun, as well as the time taken for each, and also the movement of the sun itself. At the appropriate moment its tiny brain produces the answer by which the bee can set course unerringly for home.

To make this clearer, we can translate into terms of our own everyday experience. We know, because we use clocks, that the sun rises at 6.00 hours on a particular day in the year, reaches its zenith at 12.00 hours and sets at 18.00 hours. At any time of the day we can, by looking at the position of the sun, estimate what time it is. Were we to go out walking we could take notes of our journey, writing down the times (from our wrist-watch), the length of each part of our wanderings, noting the time when we turn right or left and the distance we travelled up to that point from the place where we last noted the time. If all this were plotted on paper we should have, at the end of the journey, a complete record of our wanderings from which we could readily determine how to find our way home by reference to the sun. So far as we can tell a bee can do this without paper, pencil or wrist-watch, using the sun.

Some qualifications have had to be introduced since this marvellous discovery about bees was disclosed in 1946. For example, it now seems certain that the bees benefiting from the dances are the inexperienced foragers. The 'old hands' can find their way to the food supply by other means, including the fact that they have been there before and only need the odour from the returning bee to guide them to the flowers the dancer has visited.

Inevitably when a discovery is made in one species it is not long before other researchers notice the same thing in other species or actively test for it. Since 1946 it has been found that other animals are using polarized light from the sky to guide them. These include all insects, and also several crustaceans which do not possess such highly organized eyes as those of insects. Commensurately they do not use polarized light in the same refined ways as bees do.

The best example of a crustacean using polarized light is provided by the sandhopper, the small shrimp-like animal that jumps in all directions when rotting seaweed high up on the beach is disturbed. A sandhopper will, when the sand dries out, move towards the sea and will always go in the correct direction. It might be guided by the sight of the water or of the horizon, by the greater humidity, by taste or by smell. In fact it is guided by none of these, but uses the pattern of polarized light in the sky.

To test this, L. Pardi and F. Papi took sandhoppers from Rimini on the east coast of Italy to Gombo on the west coast. They set them down on the shore and, instead of moving towards the sea, the sandhoppers started to hop inland, following the habit they had developed on the east coast and the pattern of light associated with it.

It is difficult for us to understand this use of polarized light because it is wholly outside our experience—unless we are using it unconsciously. It has even been called the insects' sixth sense.

Daylight, other than direct sunlight, reaches us as light reflected from particles in the atmosphere. Direct sunlight is normally distributed in all directions. Light from it is polarized when its vibration is restricted to one plane only. The blue light from the sky is partly polarized. The proportion that is polarized grows less towards the sun and it also grows less in the direction away from the sun, reaching a maximum in a ring or 'equator' half way between.

Our eyes cannot appreciate this pattern, except by viewing the sky through a sheet of polaroid. Insects can do so even with no more than a little blue window through an otherwise overcast sky. The pattern depends on the position of the sun, but bees can also see the position of the sun through thick cloud because they can see the ultra-violet rays which can penetrate quite thick cloud. So presumably they have a double aid to navigation.

The truth seems to be that even those better equipped to study or understand this are still somewhat mystified. As to the part of the eye which makes use of the light, the best that can be said at present is that study of the bee's compound eye with the electron microscope suggests that it involves a regular molecular pattern in the retinal rod that runs down each ommatidium. That is, each rod is made up of innumerable tubes, each 0·000000016 mm in diameter, set at right angles to the direction of the light entering each facet of the eye.

Whatever the apparatus involved it must be relatively simple and of minute proportions since even insects with ocelli only can make use of polarized light. The caterpillars of butterflies and the larvae of sawflies have only a few ocelli on each side of the head, yet they can steer, navigate or find their way—whichever term is preferred—using polarized light.

As long ago as 1923 it had been noticed that ants could orientate their movements in relation to the sun when only a patch of blue sky was visible to them. One suggestion made was that ants could see the stars, as a man can when looking up from the bottom of a well.

An ant returning to its nest is usually following a scent trail, but it can also do so with reference to the sun and without such a trail. If it sets out from the nest with the sun to its left at right angles to its path it will return by keeping the sun to its right, and at right angles. It can also make adjustments for the movement of the sun, which it would need to do for any but the briefest journey.

One test is to pick up an ant and carry it 50 m to the right and put it down again. It will set off on its original course, even if turned the opposite way when placed on the ground, and will miss its nest by 50 m, showing that it is blindly following a compass course.

At about the time von Frisch was startling everybody with his results came another revolutionary discovery. This one was not made for one species of animal, nor by one person. The discovery was that homing birds as well as migrating birds navigate by the sun. Already in 1946 S. Dijkgraaf, in Holland, was experimenting and speculating on the subject of the orientation of migrating birds with reference to the sun.

By 1948 G. V. T. Matthews, in England, had begun to formulate a theory about the way birds could possibly navigate by the sun. There were a number of others pursuing this problem at about the same time, so navigation by the sun was very much 'in the air'. Then, in 1956, F. Sauer had the idea that some birds must navigate by the stars. After this a new term was added to the language of biology: 'celestial navigation', or navigating by the sun by day and the stars

by night. Like von Frisch's discovery, the notion of celestial navigation proved to be a breakthrough.

Bastian Schmidt had already drawn attention in 1935 to the way
his tame cuckoos became restless and perched facing south when the
time for their migration drew near. Other people since have noticed
the same phenomenon with hand-reared cuckoos and other migratory birds kept in aviaries. G. Kramer had similar experiences
while investigating the navigation of starlings, and finally he set up a
circular pavilion to test this. It was about 2 m across and 1·5 m high,
with a glass floor and six windows around the sides, the glass floor
enabling the observer to look up into the room to watch the birds'
actions. In this pavilion he put starlings which were on the point of
migrating. They settled on the perches near the window facing the
north-west, the direction they would later have gone had they been
free to migrate.

A mirror had been fitted to each window and this could be moved
to throw reflected light through the window. When the six mirrors
were set at the same angle the effect, so far as the starlings were
concerned, was to swing the sky through a right angle. The starlings
changed position to face what to them was now north-west according
to the position of the sun in the mirrors.

Nevertheless the starlings did not need to see the sun itself, and it
was clear they were responding, like the bees, to the pattern of
polarized light in the sky. With a diffuse light in the room, or with an
overcast sky overhead, the starlings were confused but could orientate themselves if they could see even a small patch of blue sky.

Matthews found his proof by accident. He was carrying out
experiments with mallard in which he found that they usually flew
in a north-westerly direction when released. Some, released shortly
after the sun had set, flew to the north-east instead. The sun had set
in the south-west, and as the birds were released a break appeared in
the clouds to the north-west and a red flush showed through. The
mallard mistook this for the setting sun and altered course to the
north-east. Such a mistake is by no means unknown. Migrating birds
have been known to be thrown off course by the red glow over a city.

During the next few years Matthews elaborated his theory,
starting with the knowledge, as shown by many experiments—his
own and other people's—that birds can appreciate the sun's movement and adjust for it at any time of the day, so keeping on their
course. He deduced that they could do this using their internal clock,
and that they also had in the brain the equivalent of a sextant.

Basically this must be true, judging solely by birds' performances.

It is the only way of explaining how a young cuckoo, that never sees its parents and flies south to Africa a month later than the parents, should follow the same course as they do. It also explains why migrating birds become confused in fog or a totally overcast sky at night and fly into lighthouses.

Birds that normally migrate from France, for example, and fly due south, will, if caught and transported 600 km to the east and there released, make no attempt to get back onto their normal route but will steadily fly on a parallel route 600 km to the east of it. The comparison with the ant transported 50 m to the right of its nest is too close to be ignored.

Although Matthews's theory has its weaknesses and its critics, we can say with confidence that birds navigate by the sun by day and the stars by night, both when migrating and homing. It is how they do it that is still not fully explained. Moreover, using similar techniques to those used for experiments with birds, it has been satisfactorily shown that celestial navigation is used by fishes, frogs and toads, and also reptiles. Whether they are using polarized light, and if so how they are using it, are questions to which there is at present no answer. It is by no means certain that human beings may not be capable of using the same means of navigation.

There are occasionally, even in the countries of western Europe, people who will as an experiment allow themselves to be blindfolded, taken by car and put down in unfamiliar terrain, after which they find their way home unaided. This faculty is said to be possessed more especially by less civilized and therefore more 'natural' people, such as the Pygmies of the Ituri Forest in the Congo, and certain tribes in Siberia. The Pygmies have been tested and there seems little doubt they can find their way back as certainly as the shearwater that was taken from Skokholm, the island off the coast of Wales, to Boston, U.S.A. in a closed hamper in a plane and there released. It returned home in twelve and a half days, having covered a distance of 5,400 km over a route it had never before travelled. Non-migratory birds can find their way back over a few kilometres only, but several migratory species have been successfully tested for distances as great as or greater than that covered by the shearwater. The times they take suggest that their return flights must have been in a straight line, and since the flights are usually over the ocean there can be little chance of the bird having used landmarks.

In 1960 E. G. F. Sauer published the results of researches he had carried out in collaboration with his wife at Freiburg in Germany. They had hatched out and hand-reared a number of warblers, small songbirds that visit Europe in spring and return to Africa in the autumn. Since they migrate almost exclusively by night Sauer was impelled to ask himself whether it could be that these and other birds that migrate by night might be able to navigate by the stars. In some ways the results of the researches of this man-and-wife team are more thrilling than any others in the field of navigation.

From the moment of hatching the warblers had been living in a sound-proof chamber, artificially lighted, so that they had no knowledge of the outside world with its sky, sun and stars. Some of them were placed in a cage with a glass top so that they could see part of the sky but nothing else of their surroundings. At the season of migration they would take up position pointing in the line of their migration flight, like compass needles. Even when their perches were rotated they kept turning back into the preferred direction. The lesser whitethroats, one species of warblers used in the experiment, kept pointing to the south-east, as they go when migrating through the Balkans and then turn south down the Nile Valley. Seemingly the only clue available to them was the night sky, and if this was obscured by cloud or in any other way they became confused. Indeed they watched the sky so intently that the appearance of a meteor made them change their direction momentarily.

The cage was then placed in a planetarium. When this was given a dim light so that no stars could be seen the warblers failed to take up their preferred direction. When the sky in the planetarium matched the sky outside precisely the birds took up their preferred direction, as if seeing the natural sky.

By changing the north–south declination of the stars in the dome of the planetarium the apparent latitude could be changed. The same could be done for the east–west declination, giving an apparent change in longitude. A lesser whitethroat was chosen for the experiment involving an artificial displacement in geography. So long as the planetarium was adjusted to the latitude in which it was sited, which was about latitude 50° north, the bird faced south-east. When it was changed along the north–south declination to 15° north, corresponding to the southern Nile valley, the bird's preferred direction was due south.

Now the east–west declination was used to move the bird seemingly from 17° longitude (Freiburg) to 77° longitude, corresponding to Lake Balkhash in Siberia. The warbler became disturbed for about a minute, looking excitedly at the sky of the planetarium, then suddenly it turned and flew westwards as if heading for its usual migration starting point at Freiburg. As the planetarium was slowly swung back, reversing the declination, so the bird shifted in direction from west to south. When the configuration of the planetarium sky was equivalent to Vienna the bird faced due south, the direction it would assume were it actually in Vienna heading for the Balkans on the first stage of its journey to Africa. By the time the planetarium sky was back to its normal for Freiburg the bird was facing south-east, the direction that would take it over the Balkans were it free to migrate.

These tests could mean only one thing, that the lesser whitethroat,

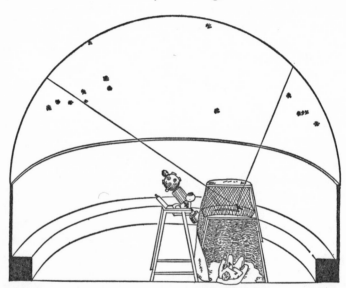

Planetarium as used by E. G. F. Sauer to study the celestial navigation of birds. The dome was 20 feet across. The sector of the sky visible to the bird in the cage is indicated by the two lines meeting at its head. A felt cloth from the bottom of the cage to the floor cuts out light from below.

without previous experience, with nothing to guide it except the stars, could orientate itself in time and space precisely to find its way to normal winter quarters in Africa. It could only mean an hereditary mechanism for relating the canopy of the sky to the geography of the earth in time and season. According to Sauer, at its very first glimpse of the sky the bird automatically adjusted its position to the direction in which it would travel.

This seems little short of miraculous, unbelievable almost, that a bird which had never been taught by its mother, had never had a chance to see the sky, let alone learn anything about it, should respond to the pattern of the stars alone with such precision. Yet all that this experiment showed was confirmed by subsequent tests. Birds migrating by day would have other clues, including landmarks if the sky were overcast. By night, in total darkness with a completely overcast sky, warblers migrating would be able only to circle help-lessly, but with a starry sky, even one partially obscured by cloud, they could follow their traditional migration routes certain of their goal.

Map illustrating Sauer's experiments with migrating warblers. The arrows show the way the birds headed for the normal migration route when the sky in the planetarium was adjusted to correspond with positions shown on the map of Europe and Asia.

Apart from the sandhopper, little attention was paid at first to whether aquatic animals might be using celestial navigation. It had been shown that the tiny fresh-water crustaceans known as water-fleas (*Daphnia*) could be made to swim in a chosen direction merely by shining a vertical beam of light onto them and changing its polarization. This was all that was known about the navigation of aquatic animals until 1950, when Talbot H. Waterman, inspired by the discoveries of von Frisch, carried out research into the direction-finding of the horseshoe crab, a marine animal that seems to use polarized light from the sky.

Celestial navigation

The horseshoe crab (*Limulus*), sometimes called the king crab, is a living fossil. Only a few species survive today, although fossils are known from as early as the Upper Carboniferous rocks 250 million years old. One of these species lives in shallow waters off the Atlantic coast of the United States. Each year these cumbersome animals come ashore at low tide to lay their eggs in the sand, after which they make their way back to the sea.

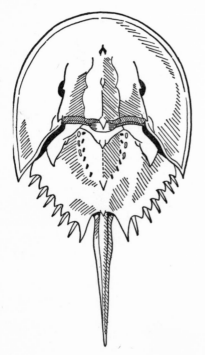

The horseshoe crab or king crab *Limulus* is a living fossil that uses celestial navigation. Since this animal has existed relatively unchanged for 250 million years we can assume that celestial navigation has been in use throughout this time.

On the top of their horseshoe-shaped shell, one on either side and directed upwards, is a pair of small kidney-shaped compound eyes. Waterman dissected out the eye and optic nerve of a freshly dead horseshoe crab, connected the nerve to a sensitive detector of electric currents and exposed the eye to a light. A polarizing filter was placed between the light and the eye and slowly rotated. Impulses in the nerve were recorded and their frequency was found to be related to the direction of polarization. In other words, *Limulus* can respond to polarized light.

Waterman then went skin-diving with a simple optical instrument capable of detecting polarized light. He found that under the sea the light is polarized in a complex pattern due to the scattering of the sun's rays by the water, but in essentials it behaved much the same as polarized light in the air. Presumably the horseshoe crab uses the polarized light from the sky as bees do, in finding its way from depths of 15 m to the water's edge, up the beach and back again, on its breeding migrations.

Since this, several investigators have tested marine fishes using less refined methods than those used on bees and birds but with similar results. Some fishes spend the nights in submarine caves, coming out each day to feed around coral reefs and returning to the caves at the end of the day. It is a relatively simple matter to catch some of these near the end of the day when they are about to return to their caves, blindfold them and set them free again. They behave as if they have completely lost their sense of direction, as they do also if an opaque sheet is held over them just above the surface of the water, or if the sky becomes suddenly overcast. Fishes caught when heading for their caves have been transported many metres to the left or right and then released back into the sea. They start swimming on the same course they were following when taken from the sea and end up as many metres to the left or right of their normal cave as they were transported. All these are characteristics of the behaviour of animals, such as bees, ants and birds, that have been demonstrated to use the polarized light of the sky to guide them.

This has a bearing on salmon migration discussed in Chapter 10. Recent researches on Pacific salmon suggest that the fishes use celestial navigation to find their way back to the coastal waters, and that it is there that they search for the smell of the water from the stream in which they were hatched.

The green turtle migrates regularly between a feeding ground and a nesting beach. These may be 2,250 km apart, but the turtles can find oceanic islands on which to lay their eggs, and tagging the turtles suggests that individual ones always return to the same beaches. That they use celestial navigation is inferred rather than proved, as it is with toads.

The common toad of Europe (*Bufo bufo*) goes to its breeding pond in spring along a well-marked route, one that has been followed for generations by its ancestors. These migration routes go straight across fields and roads, down steep banks to the roads and up steep banks on the other side. The toads travel mainly at night, walking slowly and laboriously.

During recent years there have been several instances of people buying a new house, moving in, and finding the following year that they are surrounded by hundreds of croaking toads, some of which enter the house. Inquiry has then disclosed that there was formerly a pond where the house now stands and that this was filled in to make the land available for building purposes.

It has long been a puzzle how frogs and toads scattered over the countryside could find their way back to the breeding ponds. One theory is that they are guided there by an odour from the minute algae growing in the pond. This may be true for a short range, although even that is open to argument. So far as the common toad is concerned the sense of smell seems not to be strongly developed; hardly sufficient, one would have thought, to be effective over a range of up to a mile. Nor could it be that, as with the male moth, the odour is received downwind because it not infrequently happens there are two migration routes from almost opposite directions ending at the same pond.

Preliminary results of studies made in the United States on another species suggest that the common toad, possibly also the common frog (*Rana temporaria*), though not with the same assurance, finds its way to the breeding pond as Sauer's warblers found their way to their migration routes, by the pattern of the stars in the heavens.

So far nothing has been said about the moon. Pardi and Papi, having tested their sandhoppers in daylight, went on to investigate their orientation by night. In a dark room or outside on a moonless night the sandhoppers seemed to have no particular sense of direction. When there was a moon they showed the same ability to use it as they had shown in using the day sky. They also responded to deflections in the moon's direction in a mirror and, moreover, they seemed to take into account the moon's movements across the sky.

It may be that only marine animals living on the shore respond to the moon. If so, it is a reasonable suspicion that this may be linked with the behaviour of the tides, themselves dependent on the moon.

Chapter 13

Electric biological clocks

There is a particular street corner in London where at noon every Tuesday a man used to arrive with his barrow loaded with cats' meat. Once there he would start to carve the meat for delivery to the houses around, and while carving he would throw the unwanted scraps of meat onto the ground for the cats that had assembled there. So every Tuesday, just before noon, cats could be seen arriving in anticipation. A dozen of them would gather, and they would squat on the edge of the pavement in a group, waiting for the man to come. Any other day of the week there would be no cats there, but punctually each noon on a Tuesday they would arrive to take their share of the largesse.

Plenty of people have reported that a pet dog will come to the station to meet the train on which its master is coming home from the office. The dog does this regularly and punctually. In such instances there is always the possibility that the dog may know from the small things going on around it that it is time to go to meet the train. In other words this supposed time sense in a dog may not be so much due to an internal clock as to a knowledge of events associated with the time of day.

These are only two of many examples that could be quoted and which have led people to ask whether animals have a time-sense. Scientists have also been asking themselves the same question but in a slightly different form; or, rather, they have been using a different name. They have been searching for what they call a biological clock, especially since the discovery that bees, birds and other animals were able to make allowances for movements of the sun.

There is nothing new in this except for the scientific search for the inner causes. Men have long realized that there is a rhythm in life linked with the rotation of our planet. It gives us day and night and also the seasons. Flowers open at particular times of the day, trees shed their leaves in autumn and push out their buds in spring. Some animals wake at dawn and go to sleep at dusk, others do the reverse.

All around us events are happening linked with the day, the month and the year.

One of the first recorded observations of this kind was made by Androsthenes, over two thousand years ago, in the time of Alexander the Great. Androsthenes noticed that the leaf movements of certain plants were rhythmic and followed a distinctive daily pattern. At the same period the Greek scholar, Aristotle, observed that the ovaries of sea urchins grew in size during the period of full moon. Since then there has been a long-standing belief that a number of marine animals, as well as land animals, breed at the full moon, and that certain plants crops ripen best at the full moon.

Another early observation of rhythmic behaviour was made in 1877 by a Mr Ross of Topsham, in Devon, England. He kept a shanny, a species of blenny, for several months in a sea-water aquarium. Whenever the time for high tide drew near the fish became restless. Ross noticed this and put a large stone in the aquarium with its top clear of the water. After this the shanny left the water at the time of low tide and dropped back into the water as the time of high tide approached. Although there was no movement in the water in the aquarium, and nothing else to indicate to the fish what was happening on the shore, the fish behaved always as if it knew when the tide was coming in and when it was going out.

Early in this century it began to be apparent to zoologists that all animals had an inherent rhythm of activity. This can be vividly demonstrated by the behaviour of a sea anemone, known as the plumose anemone. It is usually white and it has numerous small tentacles on its crown. If we look at a crowd of these anemones in an aquarium, at any time of the day, we see that some are completely retracted, so that they look like white buttons on the rock surface, while others are fully extended and look like beautiful white flowers. The rest will be in all manner of positions intermediate between the two. The tentacles will be at various stages of extension and retraction, and the column of the anemone's body may be shortened or lengthened, blown out like a balloon or shrunken or wrinkled, straight or leaning to one side. As we watch we may see movements in the tentacles or a slow waving of the column, and we would doubtless assume that these are movements in response to changes in the surroundings, to the presence of food or to vibrations in the water.

When a plumose anemone is kept in an aquarium without any food in the water, undisturbed by vibrations, without changes in the illumination or anything else that could impinge on it, the anemone

Plumose sea anemones in varying phases of rhythmic activity. Even without changes of any kind in their environment plumose sea anemones keep up a continuous if extremely slow round of activity, a sort of very slow-motion ballet.

will go through all the positions we have noted, in a kind of slow-motion ballet. There are times when, under natural conditions, a disturbance in the water or food swimming by will make the anemone contract or push out its body or its tentacles. Nevertheless under constant conditions there is this continuous rhythmic sequence. A similar rhythmic sequence has been demonstrated in other animals. We experience it ourselves and it is best shown when we are asleep, to all intents completely at rest, yet we know that we move and turn in bed throughout the night.

About twenty years ago it was discovered that certain small mammals, including mice and shrews, showed alternating periods of sleep and activity every three hours during the day and night. We had long been familiar with the idea that some animals were diurnal, that is, active by day, and others are active by night, or nocturnal. Such divisions have, however, proved to be only broad generalizations. For example, some bats are on the wing for an hour or two at dusk and nightfall, then go back to their roost and come out again for an hour or two just before dawn. We speak of these as crepuscular.

In place of these ideas of diurnal and nocturnal animals, we tend now to think in terms of what an animal does during each twenty-four hours, and here it has been found that all animals so far investigated, if kept under constant conditions such as those in which the plumose anemone was kept, have a rhythm that varies between twenty-two and twenty-seven hours. This is called the circadian rhythm, from the Latin *circa*, about, and *dies*, a day.

This internal rhythm has to be seen as an internal clock which keeps bad time, so that it can lose or gain an hour or two each day. It is, however, kept right by external circumstances. For example, a particular species of bird may awaken at dawn and will do so punctually. If kept under experimental conditions it will not be so punctual about going to sleep. In a natural state, however, the fading light tells it that the time has come to go to roost. Its internal rhythm is, therefore, kept in check and corrected each day by the length of daylight.

Instances occur in which an important action takes place at twenty-four-hourly intervals. The fruit fly *Drosophila* that is used so much in the laboratory emerges from the pupa in the early hours of the morning, when under natural conditions the air would be moist and the temperature low. When the adult insect leaves the pupal case its cuticle is soft and not yet waterproof. If it came out when the air is dry and the temperature is high it would run the risk of being dried up. Therefore a twenty-four-hour timing, so that the insect leaves the pupa about dawn, is almost a necessity. Under laboratory conditions, with the air kept moist and at a fairly low temperature, this twenty-four-hour timing is still maintained.

Another familiar activity that takes place at approximately twenty-four-hour intervals is egg-laying. Most birds lay one egg a day until the clutch is complete, at about twenty-four-hour intervals. Heart-beat and body temperature also vary rhythmically throughout the twenty-four hours, and it has been shown that the domestic fowl has more red cells in its blood at midnight than at noon and that the number varies rhythmically throughout each twenty-four hours, and the same is true of the white blood cells.

Marine animals living between tide-marks are immersed in water or exposed to air for alternating periods each day. As the tide goes out many of them take action that will prevent them from drying out. A limpet, for example, clings so tightly to the rock surface at low-tide that the supply of water trapped under its shell, which keeps the limpet's body moist and supplies oxygen for breathing, cannot leak away. When the tide is in the limpet leaves its 'home' on the rock face and wanders over to a patch of green seaweed to feed. It must, however, return home before the tide goes out. Only very rarely do we see a limpet returning home after the water has receded down the beach.

These animals must adjust their behaviour to the rise and fall of the tides, which vary by about an hour each day. So a regular rhythm is useless to them. They must have one that anticipates the changing times of the tides. Moreover when placed in an aquarium, in which they are covered all the time by water, they will continue to behave as if the tide were rising and falling, at least for a while.

The fiddler crab shows a different reaction to the tidal rhythm. Some species are darker when first exposed at low water and are light in colour at high tide. The changes, which continue in an aquarium, are due to expansion and contraction of pigment cells in the skin. If pieces of tissue containing these pigment cells are taken from the crab and kept alive for several weeks they will continue to show the same expansion and contraction, and therefore will change colour in tune with the tides.

This leads to the suspicion that even individual cells take part in the time-keeping.

The particular fiddler crab *Uca* studied in these experiments also showed other rhythms. Two were concerned with respiration, one showing a maximum intake of oxygen at the time of the low tide, the other showing a maximum intake between 03.00 and 05.00 hours and a minimum between 16.00 and 18.00 hours.

Another kind of rhythm is that seen in the lugworm. The only people who see this worm are fishermen, who dig it out of the sand to use it as bait, and inquisitive naturalists. Otherwise all we see is the piles of worm casts on the sandy beach at low tide and, a few inches from each pile, a saucer-shaped depression in the sand. Each pile of castings and its adjacent depression represent the openings of a U-shaped burrow beneath the surface, in which a lugworm is living.

At forty-minute intervals, with great regularity, the lugworm moves in its burrow. It moves its tail end to the surface to discharge its faeces as the worm cast. Then it moves back to the bottom of the burrow where by vigorous wave movements of its body it draws in water from the hole in the saucer-shaped depression for breathing. Every seven minutes it pushes out its proboscis towards the depression to take sand into its mouth for feeding, extracting from the sand the particles of dead plant and animal matter.

When taken into the laboratory and placed in a U-shaped glass tube, in an aquarium, the lugworm continues these two rhythmic movements, even with no food available to it. Moreover if the head end is cut off and suspended in sea water a series of gentle waves continue to flow through the gullet and with each wave the proboscis gives a rhythmic outburst. If the gullet is then severed from the proboscis the waves continue in its wall but cease in the proboscis, so the pacemaker controlling the rhythm must be in the wall of the gullet.

This can be compared, approximately, with the household refrigerator, which shows long periods of inactivity broken by short periods of activity. The pacemaker in this case is the thermostat which switches on the motor when the temperature reaches a certain level. In the lugworm no change of temperature is needed: the action is spontaneous.

The lugworm's rhythm is of forty-minute periodicity, but there is the same appearance of spontaneity in yearly rhythms, as shown by the further experiments of E. G. F. Sauer. He hatched and hand-reared warblers (see Chapter 12), that are summer residents in Europe, in soundproof chambers artificially lighted so that they had the equivalent of perpetual summer. Had they been living in the wild they would have responded to natural cues, such as the shortening day, to migrate to Africa for the southern summer. Yet although they were completely cut off from any such cues they became restless in autumn. They flitted from branch to branch in their artificial home and were wakeful at night. Had they been able to migrate they would have been on the wing all night. This restlessness continued for about the time it would have taken them to fly to Africa. Then they resumed normal habits, including sleeping at night. In the spring, when the free warblers were migrating back to Europe, the incarcerated warblers, still in an unchanging environment, again became restless and wakeful at night. Sauer remarked that it was as if they had an inner clock which told them when to take wing for the annual migration. Had they been exposed to cues in a natural environment their internal rhythm would have been translated into migration. As it was, Sauer had produced acceptable evidence that there is an internal rhythm that is wholly divorced from what is going on around the birds.

Probably the best known yearly rhythm is that of the palolo worm, of the South Pacific. This lives in holes and crevices in coral reefs and each year the sex organs mature at the third quarter of the moon in October and again in November. Then the rear half of the body, containing the reproductive organs, breaks away and swims to the surface, the front half remaining in the reef to repeat the spawning the following year. So precise is the time when these ripe halves swarm to the surface that the local people can go out in their canoes to scoop them up for their annual feast.

On the Pacific coast of the United States a similar event has attracted attention. On the exceptionally high tides that occur twice a month, from March to June, grunion, small fishes 15 cm long, swarm up the beach just after the tide has turned on the second, third and fourth nights after the full moon. The females, carried just out of the water by an incoming wave, dig in the sand with their tails and lay their eggs, the males following to fertilize them. Then both slip back into the sea. The eggs are not again wetted until the high tide two weeks later, when they hatch and the fish larvae slip back into the sea.

Enough has been said to illustrate the various rhythms, which depend on a biological clock of unknown identity. It is time now to turn to the experimental search for something nearer to what most people regard as a true time-sense.

Cockroaches are unwelcome in the house, but they have been much used for laboratory work on the internal clock. They become active a little before dark, and their activity reaches a peak a few hours later then dies down to a low level half way through the night. Suppose cockroaches are kept experimentally in the dark from 18.00 hours until 06.00 hours the following morning, after which they are subjected to light for twelve hours. Then, one day, the light is switched on at midnight.

In a natural state changes in time of nightfall are gradual, so the cockroach's internal clock adjusts to them. If, experimentally, the hour of darkness—started by switching off the laboratory lights—is advanced six hours in one day, and this is continued on the following days, the cockroaches do not respond by becoming active six hours earlier straight away. They change their times by a relatively small amount each day, namely one and a half hours, so that they adjust to the six-hour change in four days.

If the time is altered by larger amounts, advancing the hour of darkness by ten or twelve hours, the cockroaches become completely confused.

All this suggests that cockroaches have an internal clock that can adjust only to relatively small changes in the external world. These are more especially changes in illumination, but temperature changes can also be important. Apart from this the clock is largely independent and self-regulating.

Many of the results of researches on cockroaches tend to be contradictory, which is to be expected from the intricacy and complexity of the operations involved. They can, however, be satisfactorily summarized to date. From two cells only in the brain, impulses pass along the main nerve cord to nerve ganglia in the thorax controlling the legs. When a cockroach comes out of its dark hiding-place, where it has been resting during the day, it is because these two cells have sent a message to the ganglia in the thorax and these set the legs in motion.

Obviously this is an over-simplification, but it represents the fundamentals of the awakening process. Hormones are given out at some point in this process and it is the balance between how much the nerves contribute to the awakening and how much is determined by hormones that has caused the contradictory results to arise.

That hormones are involved is shown by experiments in which body fluids from one cockroach injected into another cockroach can alter its clock. Thus a cockroach is trained by altering the time at which its illumination is switched on to be several hours later in awaking. When a small drop of its body fluid is transferred to a cockroach behaving normally, this second cockroach starts to be several hours late in waking.

This has been taken further by producing what are called arrhythmic individuals. Cockroaches reared and kept in continuous darkness are continually active (or arrhythmic) throughout the twenty-four hours. During that time the total of their activity is no greater than in those experiencing a regular day and night, but it is more evenly spread. An arrhythmic cockroach can have its internal clock readjusted by an injection of the body fluid from a normal cockroach, after which it rests for twelve hours and is active for twelve hours, more or less, in each twenty-four hours.

An arrhythmic cockroach can also be made rhythmic by exposing it to a brief flash of light. Even if it is still kept in total and continuous darkness it will then continue with the normal twelve hours rest and twelve hours activity as it would have done had it lived a normal life from the moment of hatching. A prolonged exposure to light, however, merely confuses the cockroach.

So far as daily rhythms are concerned, the numerous researches on a wide variety of animals all show similar results. They give the impression of a mechanism inside the animal that behaves remarkably like that inside a man-made clock except that it has greater powers of self-adjustment.

As long ago as 1908 A. Forel described how he had watched bees coming to the table for jam at regular times. He noticed one day that a single bee came to the jam. The next day several bees came. Jam was on the table at breakfast and tea time only, never at lunch or supper, although other food was on the table. Although in the first few days after this the bees turned up at each meal, they then took to visiting the table only at breakfast and tea time. It looked, therefore, as though the bees had not just happened to fly in because they saw the table laid but had learned the times of meals and had also learned when jam would be on the table.

Forel tested the bees. He arranged for no jam to be put on the table at any meal. The bees still came at breakfast and tea time, and seemed obviously to be searching for the jam as they crawled into cups and other crockery.

Other people have carried out similar experiments since 1908, and nothing they have done undermines the results obtained by Forel. Ingeborg Beling kept a hive of bees in a room in conditions of constant illumination, humidity and temperature. She found bees could easily be trained to visit a dish of sugared water at certain times of the day and during the night as well.

Beling's bees were not reacting to small changes in the environment because there were none. Other people have tested bees to see whether, like the dog going to the station to meet its master, their time-keeping was internal or external. One experiment is to take a bee trained to go to sugared water at certain times and subject it to a low temperature for an hour or so. This slows down its metabolism and the bee is then late in visiting the syrup. Drugs have been used. One drug that increases the rate of metabolism makes the bee arrive early at the syrup. Another drug that depresses the rate of metabolism makes it arrive late. Experimenters have gone into even greater detail by chilling only the part of the brain where the two cells of the pacemaker are lodged—a rather delicate operation!—with the result that the insect arrives late at its feeding bowl.

In a way all such experiments could be regarded as a waste of effort, because anyone who is a field naturalist soon begins to realize how regularly animals behave. If he sees a green woodpecker feeding on the lawn at 13.00 hours one day he may expect to see it at that same time the next day. Either that or it will not come at all that day because it is visiting another feeding ground. It was regularity of this sort that caused one naturalist to say to another, years ago, that birds were not 'free as air' as the poets would have us believe, but creatures of habit as tied to a routine as anyone working in an office or a factory.

Bees can be seen visiting a particular kind of flower at 11.00 hours each day and another kind of flower at 15.00 hours, because those are the times these particular flowers open. A man who feeds the pigeons every morning when he arrives to open the factory door will find them waiting for him when he arrives.

We have already seen how a bee or a bird uses the movements of the sun in its daily activities. Now we need to find out how this sun clock is related to the biological clock. This has been tested especially with the common starling. It is possible to train this bird to select food from the one box of a ring of boxes that lies to the north. It needs the sun to be able to do this, and at any time of the day that it needs to feed it will go to this north box, using the sun as a guide. This suggests the possibility that the clock controlling this is the same as the one that controls its activity as a whole, its biological clock.

An experiment was devised to test this. Two starlings were trained, one to go to the north box, the other to go to a box facing west. Then both were kept in conditions of continuous illumination in place of the normal day and night. Instead of starting to be active at dawn, as they would under natural circumstances, the time when they began to be active became earlier and earlier. After this had gone on for several days the two birds were once more tested with their feeding boxes. Each one consistently chose the wrong box, to the left of the correct one. When, however, they were returned to a normal cycle of day and night, and were again allowed to choose their feeding boxes, each went once more without hesitation to the correct box. This suggests strongly that the clock responsible for compensating for the sun's movement is the same as that governing the daily rhythm of activity.

Another approach was made to this problem by taking the sand-hoppers, used in the experiments described in Chapter 12, to the southern hemisphere. They were flown to South America from Italy. There they used the sun's movements to find their way down the beach just as they would have done in Italy, although everything around them was different. Their internal clock was behaving as unalterably as the wrist watches carried by the people who took them there.

A mole spends practically all its time underground, yet its day of twenty-four hours is divided into alternating four-hourly spells of rest and activity. If you see the earth of a molehill heaving at 11.00 hours one day, it is fairly certain that you will see this happening, in that molehill or one adjacent to it, the next day at 11.00 hours.

Animals living underground, or going underground to rest, cannot rely on daylight to wake them up. Some small rodents actually seal the entrance to the burrow when they retire to sleep, yet wake unfailingly as darkness falls. Bats, and birds such as swiftlets and oilbirds that sleep in caves in absolute darkness, and need to use echo-location to move about in the caves, must clearly have an internal clock. Bats especially need an internal clock because not only are they cut off from daylight and the changes that go with night and day but their body temperature drops when they sleep to only a few degrees above that of the surrounding air. To awake punctually at dusk, therefore, their bodies must start warming up in advance.

There is nothing remarkable in this when we remember that people of regular habits will wake promptly at 06.00 hours, shall we say, without any auxiliary aid. Indeed we know from experience that a person wishing to get up at an unusual hour the following morning has only to register this in his mind on going to bed and he will awaken at the stated hour. This is something I have often done, and if it is argued that one is made aware of what hour it is by the sounds from the world around I would instance the occasion when I 'willed' myself to wake the following morning at 05.00 hours. When I awoke it was to hear the clock on the landing outside my bedroom strike 04.00 hours. Being already out of bed and fully awake, however, I continued. It transpired that the clock, unknown to me, was an hour slow!

J. Aschoff and J. Meyer-Lohmann set out to trace when, in the life of an animal, the biological clock begins to tick. They placed chicks of the domestic fowl, as soon as they hatched, in cages under constant conditions, so that there was no appearance of night and day, nor any changes in temperature and humidity. At first, as was to be expected, the movements of the chicks were feeble, but as they grew stronger so an orderly rhythm became apparent. This became more and more evident from the third to the eleventh day, when a true circadian rhythm could be registered of just over twenty-five hours.

Nevertheless other rhythms within the body of a chick can be detected even before it hatches. Long before the shell is broken a chick must breathe, and it does so using oxygen that diffuses through the shell. By measuring the rate of this diffusion F. Barnwell and L. Johnson detected a distinct rhythm in the oxygen used up. More-over although the chick cannot see, and only the very slightest changes in light would be seen through the shell anyway, there was a markedly greater consumption of oxygen during daylight hours than at night.

In 1969 A. G. Azaryan and V. P. Tyschenko pinpointed the neurons in the protocerebrum of crickets as the mechanism controlling circadian rhythms. They ligatured between the head and thorax of the cricket, so preventing the movement of neurosecretory granules without interfering with the nerves. The biological clock was not upset. The nerve impulses in the protocerebrum had a daily rhythm which corresponded with the increase and decrease in the insect's activity. These impulses were directly affected by the changes from day to night and vice versa. They acted as a trigger to the nerve ganglia controlling the movements of the insect's legs. In this way, it seems, the cricket's activity is directly synchronized with the day/night cycle of illumination.

Perhaps the last word can be said by those who have studied the crayfish *Orconectes pellucidus* which lives in lightproof underground caves, where the temperature never varies and the environment is as constant in all its features as in any laboratory experiment. This species has been living under these conditions for between 25,000 and half a million years, yet it shows not only the rhythms of respiration and others like it, which we would expect, but it also preserves a circadian rhythm, a biological clock that still goes on ticking although the need for it has passed long ago.

Summing up all the evidence, of which only a very small part has been presented here, it seems that all organisms can count the days, months and years, that in their bodies they have small rhythms and larger rhythms, the smaller controlled by the larger and the larger controlled by the largest, inevitably recalling the wheels in a clock, the second hands being the cells themselves. All that is lacking is the pendulum, the pacemaker keeping everything under control. We know this control operates partly through the nerves, partly through hormones. But opinion seems to be favouring the theory that time-keeping is an electrical mechanism, and if this can be confirmed the future strategy of research will be radically different from that pursued during the last twenty years.

Beside all this it seems mere child's play for a few cats to be able to know when it is noon on Tuesday, to assemble at a street corner for titbits.

Chapter 14

Necklaces of behaviour

Our boxer dog was several months old when he experienced his first thunderstorm. After the first clap of thunder he went to an open door and looked out. Knowing how most dogs become frightened during a thunderstorm, I went and stood beside him, looking down at him, ready to comfort and reassure him if he should show signs of fear. So I was all set to observe what happened at the next thunderclap. The lightning was not very obvious to us and seemed not to affect him. Then, as the sound of the thunder rolled across the sky, from left to right, I saw the dog's reactions in detail. His ears were pricked, listening intently. He sniffed the air. His whiskers bristled and his head turned from left to right in time with the passage of the rumbling, as if watching. This was the first time I had been made aware of a very elementary principle in the study of animal behaviour, that an animal brings all its senses to bear on an unfamiliar object or event.

The reason for recounting this episode is that we, who so predominantly use our eyes to examine a new situation, tend to think of the senses in isolation. For the purpose of setting forth the study of animal senses in a book, it is necessary to deal with each one separately. We have chapters on taste, smell, touch, hearing and vision, because to do otherwise would cause confusion. At the end of this, however, it is essential to show that in life they are not separated in this arbitrary manner, as my boxer taught me so vividly.

About a year after this thunderstorm occurred I was asked to take over the care of a genet. This is an African animal related to mongooses but looking like a slender and extremely graceful tabby cat, with large ears, fairly large eyes, a pointed snout and long whiskers. We had prepared a small room for our new guest, bare of anything except for branches arranged round the upper part of the room and with several leading up to these from the floor. Since a genet hunts a great deal in shrubs and trees, this was likely to make it feel at home and give it appropriate exercise.

When the genet was first put down in the room it made a dash up the wall and onto the window. As its claws failed to engage on the glass of the window and it started to slip backwards, it twisted its whole body and landed on one of the horizontal branches. Having been thwarted in its first dash for freedom it rested for a while surveying its new home, looking around with its delicate ears vibrating and its whiskers twitching. Then it started to explore the room.

From the start, moving very, very slowly, it put a forepaw onto the branch to test it, before lifting another foot. Having made sure that the branch would not give way under its foot it advanced a hindpaw, again testing the branch before moving the next forepaw. So the genet progressed all round the room, infinitely slowly, testing with each foot as it went. All the time its other alert senses were at work. It stretched its head forward, moved it from side to side and up and down, its whiskers twitching all the time, its nostrils moving as it sniffed, its mobile ears moving this way and that and vibrating all the time, and its eyes intent on every small detail.

The walls of the room were bare except for an occasional cobweb, and here and there were blemishes and spots on the distemper. None of these small details escaped the genet. It examined each spot, each blemish, each cobweb with its nose, presumably after having used its eyes to see it, and all the time its ears, nostrils and whiskers were on the move.

Having completed a tour of the room in this painstakingly slow motion, the genet reached its starting point and began a second slow tour of the room, following precisely the same route, and again with every sense concentrated on examining the details of its surroundings, and every footstep being used to test the ground or the branch it was on before lifting another foot.

At the end of this second tour, and in marked contrast to the other two tours, the genet raced round the room at high speed, along precisely the same route. It looked as if the genet, having made its two slow-motion inspections, had memorized every detail of the topography of the room and could now travel at high speed with perfect confidence.

Genets are nocturnal, and during the nights that followed—and for years afterwards—we would hear it dashing about along the branches and over the floor of the room, never once falling, so far as we could tell. Since the window was small and the first nights were moonless, there could have been little light entering the room. The genet must, therefore, have been finding its way around the room using to a large extent memories stored during that first inspection.

Later the genet was given an outdoor enclosure, its walls and ceiling of wire-netting, furnished with branches as in its indoor room. The window was opened to allow the animal to pass from the indoor room to the outdoor enclosure. The first time it was able to go into the outdoor enclosure it repeated the tactics employed in inspecting the indoor room. It first went up and down the branches, and along each one as well as over the ground, infinitely slowly, one paw at a time, looking around and sniffing, its ears vibrating and its whiskers twitching. Having completed the circuit it went over it a second time at the same painfully slow pace, and followed this by racing at top speed all around the enclosure.

One small incident suggested how great a part memory plays in the lives of animals. On the first inspection, in spite of the care with which it was carried out, the genet slipped at a particular place along one of the branches and recovered its position by swinging under the branch, gripping with all four feet, and jerking itself back onto the upper surface of the branch, as a gymnast would do on a horizontal bar. For ever afterwards the genet on reaching this particular spot would perform this same somersault.

We know that young mammals, as they are becoming independent of the parent, first move around near the nest, gradually increasing the area they cover each day, until finally they wander away never to return. Were it possible to follow their movements closely, as I could do with the genet, we should find, almost certainly, the same inspection of the terrain. The only difference between their performance and that of the genet would be that young animals would be gradually learning their way about instead of, like the genet, having to telescope their education into a short space of time. This learning must be especially valuable to nocturnal animals who although they have night vision probably depend far more on their other senses, in combination, than we normally realize.

By comparison with the elegant research carried out in laboratories such observations seem almost out of date. Yet they still have a value, if only in helping us always to remember that animals' senses do not work in isolation. The turtles that cross a thousand kilometres of sea to visit their breeding beaches are believed by some scientists to use celestial navigation, as mentioned in Chapter 12, but to pretend that this is the whole story would be to delude. A. Koch, A. Carr and D. Ehrenfeld have recently given attention to the green turtles visiting Ascension Island to lay their eggs after having spent their time feeding off Brazil. They suggest that Ascension Island emits some kind of chemical trail that is carried by the South Equatorial current flowing past the island. This current is 1,600 km wide and never more than 60 m deep, so any chemical in the water will not move much up and down and would only be diluted a hundred, at most a thousand, times as it spread sideways. It must therefore be possible, they have argued, for a turtle to pick up the scent even if it had to dive to 60 m depth to the boundary between the water containing the Ascension Island odour and the other oceanic water in order to be sure it was on the right trail.

Given these considerations, all a turtle would need then would be a simple compass sense, which it would obtain by noting the position of the sun. Even this celestial navigation together with following a scent trail in the water may not be sufficient to take the turtle from the feeding area to the egg-laying beach. When, for example, the young turtles hatch from the eggs buried deep in the sand they climb up towards the surface, but they do not climb out until nightfall. Were they to do so they would be in even greater danger. So many enemies, from crabs and sea-birds to predatory fishes, are waiting to capture them.

The baby turtle does not stay under the surface because it knows there is danger, but because it becomes lethargic in temperatures higher than 28·5° C. By day the surface of the sand is hotter than this except in the early morning, by which time the turtles hatching out the day before will be safely in the sea, or when it rains, when at least some of its enemies will be at a disadvantage. Once it has left the sand it makes its way to the sea in a direct line, by-passing any obstacles such as a log washed ashore. Young turtles appear to be more attracted to blue or green light, the colours of the sea, than to those of the land, but tests have shown that it is brightness, not colour, that attracts them, and that it is the brightness of a distant horizon that beckons them in the direction of the sea.

It has also been shown incidentally to the researches carried out on baby turtles that within the range of 25–31° C. the warmer the water the less active they are. This is another advantage in making the journey to the sea at night: the baby turtles will find the temperature of the sea most favourable for their swimming.

There is reason to believe that the adult green turtle swims most strongly at temperatures of 25° C. This may be another reason for its migrations in the South Equatorial Current, which for most of its course has a mean isotherm of 25–26° C. To north and south of it the isotherms are lower than this. So, conceivably, temperature is important in deciding its migration.

N. Mrosovsky, who has played a leading part in researches on the green turtle, has remarked that probably a chain of reactions to different stimuli is involved in getting the baby turtles safely into the sea and across to the feeding ground. He has called this a 'necklace of behaviour'—descriptive phrase! The return journey of the turtle to lay eggs probably involves another necklace, and since such a necklace must involve several senses it bears comparison with what was seen in my genet and boxer.

A simple example of a necklace of behaviour can be seen in the egg-laying of an ichneumon fly. The female lays her eggs in the wood-boring larvae of a particular sawfly. To lay an egg in the larva of any other species would be a waste of time since the larva from it would fail to develop. It would also be a waste of time if the ichneumon laid her egg in a sawfly larva that already contained the egg of an ichneumon fly.

The female ichneumon is guided as she runs over the bark of a tree to a spot where the sawfly larva is feeding in its tunnel. Her organs of smell are in her feet. She can tell from the odour emanating from the larva whether or not it contains an egg already. Assuming the larva has not already been parasitized she now needs to listen for the sound of it wriggling in its tunnel. The sense of touch is then used to insert the ovipositor. The probability is that other senses are used as well in what used to be thought of as a relatively simple operation. Even to

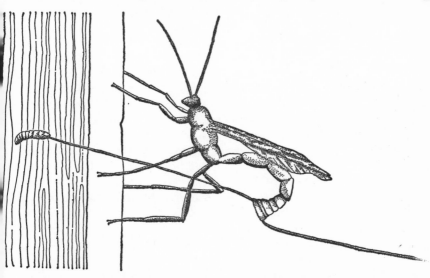

Female ichneumon fly inserting her long needle-like ovipositor into the side of a tree. This fly lays its eggs in the bodies of wood-boring grubs. Even this apparently simple operation depends for success on an exquisite combination of senses.

161

have elucidated these few components has called for a number of separate pieces of research, each demanding a high degree of skill. Others may one day be revealed, perhaps by accident, as happened in the case of the common swift which comes to Europe for a short summer season to breed.

This bird has long been known as an indicator of bad weather and has often been called the storm-swallow, rain-swallow and thunder-bird as a consequence. Swifts stand out as skilled aviators which spend all their time on the wing, hunting tiny insects at speeds of 160 km per hour, even roosting on the wing. In heavy rain insects disappear from the air and swifts cannot afford even a short interruption in their hunting if they are to feed themselves and their nestlings.

At one moment the sun is shining and the swifts are flying overhead in all directions, then storm clouds appear. The sky becomes overcast, passing from grey to black, and we see the swifts streaming away usually to the south or south-west. Soon after the last birds have disappeared from sight the storm breaks, with torrential rains, lightning and thunder. After the storm has passed the swifts return. Meanwhile their nestlings go into a state resembling hibernation until the parents return to feed them.

The movements of the swifts in space have been well studied, so that we know they become aware of approaching cyclonic storms when these are as much as 1,300 km away. The meteorological disturbance is hardly greater than the disturbance it causes to the swifts themselves. Sometimes the disturbances last several days, the swifts withdrawing from the area, flying against the wind as much as 800 km from their nests, returning again when the storm has passed.

It seems incredible that birds so intent on chasing tiny insects, needing all their senses on the alert not only to snap these up while travelling at high speed, but also to avoid collision with one another, should become aware of storms moving at such a distance from them. Whether they are made aware by air pressures, vibrations or electrical discharges, by sight, hearing or by some special sense of which we are unaware, has yet to be learned. Few scientists have bothered even to speculate on this. Then there is the journey itself, which may be 1,600 km there and back. The initial stages of this, at the least, are often made when the sky and sun are totally obscured, when the use of solar navigation must be at a minimum. Nevertheless, as with the shearwater returning from Boston, the swifts must get their bearings from the heavens, unless their vision is so acute they can, from the heights at which they fly, pick out landmarks that guide them on their return journey.

The questions have to be asked before they can be answered, and not infrequently the sheer interest of one aspect can deflect attention over a long period from other, more subsidiary, aspects. This, probably, is why so many questions about bats remain unanswered: we have been so taken up with the sheer wonder of the world of echo-location revealed to us that we tend to concentrate on their sense of hearing to the exclusion of their other senses, which are used in conjunction with it.

Bats are notoriously odorous, and their roosts are even more so, a point that is seldom noted by those writing on the biology of bats. Beneath the skin of the snout are large glands causing conspicuous folds round the lips and nose. These are formed by sebaceous glands which in other mammals produce the oil that keeps the coat waterproof. In the case of bats, each of these glands has a long bristle springing from it, which may act in some way as a sense-organ. There are similar glands on the neck and elsewhere on the body in some species. These are the glands that produce the rancid odour, which may be used for recognition between individual bats, or it may be that the scent trail left by a flying bat helps in keeping groups of bats in touch with one another. It seems inconceivable also that the rank odour of the roost should serve no purpose, and the most obvious one to suggest would be that it helps the bats to find their way back.

Within a roost bats hang upside-down, holding on by their toes, using the slightest cracks in the ceiling of a cave, hollow tree or building. Each bat has its favoured spot—one might almost say favoured crevice—for its toehold. It has been suggested that a bat roosting in a cave may find its way to its toehold by counting the number of wing-beats from the cave entrance to the roosting spot. There it must use a delicacy of touch such as only blind people possess or can appreciate, to find its toehold in that split second between the act of turning upside-down in flight and folding its wings.

Horseshoe bats hibernate in caves, but they do not sleep solidly during the winter. Should the temperature fall below a certain level a bat will awake, fly around inside the cave and find another place to hang from. If the temperature outside the cave rises to 10° C. or more a hibernating bat will wake and fly out to feed on dung beetles that are active in winter. Clearly there is a fine sensitivity to temperature changes felt while the animal is in the profound sleep, near to death, of hibernation. This sensitivity, as we have already seen, is demonstrated by the way a sleeping bat, hanging from the ceiling of a cave, will swing its whole body sideways away from a finger held towards it.

There are records of banded horseshoe bats being noted in one cave in the early days of hibernation and then found later in the winter in another cave over 30 km away. The reason why they should do this is unknown, and so is their method of navigation. Perhaps they use the stars or the moon. Noctules and other bats are known to make migrations of up to 750 km. Some of these flights are made by day and at fair heights, so it must be suspected that the bats are using solar navigation.

If this sounds improbable, so did a story from a South African mine many years ago. Unfortunately the species of bat involved was not recorded, but the rest of the story is of interest in view of later research. The story was that mine inspectors noticed how bats flying along the galleries would stop squeaking when the lights were switched on, and would resume when they were switched off. Some pulses used in echo-location, although ultrasonic, have components heard as clicks or buzzes at the lower end of the frequency scale. Griffin and others had experimented with bats flying in full light and had found no evidence that bats used vision to find their way around. Then in 1967 J. N. Lane of Cornell University, and two years later, J. W. Bradbury and F. Nottebolim, in further experiments, found that bats do use vision, but only in dim light. They found that in strong light the bats had to use their echo-location, but in dim light, the kind of light one would expect in the illuminated galleries of a mine, they could avoid obstacles even when their ears were plugged.

The way of life of a nocturnal animal can only be painfully and laboriously pieced together, largely because we, the investigators, rely so much on vision and daylight. The task is even more difficult when we have to deal with animals living wholly underground. A mole, for example, moves restlessly about a system of tunnels of more or less rectangular design lying 7 to 45 cm under the surface. At frequent intervals this network has a shaft going to the surface where there is a molehill, and also at intervals there are shafts running like spiral staircases without steps to 1 m or more deep. All these tunnels are little more than 5 cm in diameter.

Mole-catchers know that if a mole's tunnel is blocked the animal will make a detour. It will make a side-tunnel which bypasses the obstruction and links up exactly with the old tunnel. It is the precision with which the new tunnel joins the old one that is so remarkable. There have been instances in which a mole, released on the surface 2 to 3 m away from its known tunnel system, has dug down into the ground and driven a new tunnel to reach its pre-existing tunnel and, again, this has precisely joined the old tunnel. Observations like these have led to zoologists speaking of a mole's sense of orientation.

Schematic drawing showing how moles and mole-like rodents can tunnel with precision. In real life and in laboratory tests moles and other tunnellers have shown a surprising ability to make new borings connect precisely with the old. When a run is blocked the animal bores a fresh tunnel to connect precisely beyond the blockage.

F. C. Eloff has investigated the sense of orientation of golden moles and mole-rats in southern Africa. Both burrow underground and both have the general form of a mole. They lack eyes and external ears, one of the main differences between them being that whereas true moles and golden moles both dig with their forefeet, the mole-rat digs with its front teeth. They are, however, all sufficiently alike in their way of life for us reasonably to suppose that they use their senses in much the same way.

A mole-rat burrows only 7 to 10 cm under the surface, and its tunnels must be frequently damaged by hoofs and heavy rains. When Eloff deliberately damaged a length of tunnel the mole-rat would block the entrance to the damaged portion, then, from the undamaged part, dig a short lateral tunnel, turn left or right and continue parallel to the old tunnel, turning in to join with it at a point just beyond the farthest end of the damaged part. If left undisturbed the mole-rat would later remake the damaged tunnel, but if the new lateral tunnel were then blocked it would repeat the operation of driving another tunnel parallel to the old one. If necessary it would repeat this a dozen times, always making the lateral tunnels accurately join the old one.

Eloff tested females with their underground nests and found that they would always burrow unerringly to the nest no matter from which direction they started and no matter how many times their tunnels were blocked. He commented: '. . . where such damage occurs proper connection between even widely-separated, undisturbed tunnel sections is effected in a remarkably short time and correct manner, while at the same time the mole displays highly-developed powers of orientation.' Other experiments carried out on the European mole supports these findings.

In this situation it is not difficult to enumerate the signals available to these burrowing animals. First there will be virtually no light, except possibly where a vertical shaft opens to the surface, and this would be at most extremely dim. Secondly, temperature would be constant at any depth below 5 to 7 cm. We are then left with sounds, vibrations and air currents.

The ground is made up of strata of differing densities, with streams and rivers traversing it as well as springs and underground streams. Throughout there will be burrows and tunnels of many kinds that are permanent, at least for the lifetime of a mole, through which air currents will flow. Even gentle winds across the mouths of these will contribute noises and vibrations, not least in the mole's own tunnel system. The width of a mole tunnel is hardly more than the diameter of the animal's body. A mole has no external ears, but it is in a similar position to that of a man putting his ear to the ground, in that the side of its head must be always close to the wall of the tunnel. A plumber will put the head of a hammer to the floor of a house near a water-pipe, and put his ear near the other end of the handle to detect a small leak in a water pipe somewhere in the house. A mole is virtually doing this all the time.

The earth will smell differently from place to place and from one spot to another, according to the dampness or dryness and the various types of vegetation. It is not too extravagant to suppose that a mole or a mole-rat will carry a memory of its earthy world in the form of a pattern of smells, sounds and vibrations, just as certainly as we carry a memory of streets and houses, or of roads, fields and trees. A sense of orientation cannot be other than a combination of the workings of several senses, including touch, which, as we saw in Chapter 2, is highly developed in a mole.

I once went to call on a friend a mile away. I had a problem I was trying to solve. I suddenly awoke to the fact that I was at my friend's front door, but I could recall nothing of my journey, although at one point I had had to cross a busy main road and this was before the days of pedestrian crossings. Apparently with the mind so fully occupied that my conscious self had been oblivious of all around, my senses had guided me faultlessly.

There is no telling how many people may have had to step aside to avoid a collision with me, or what would have happened had some inconspicuous barrier been erected on what for me was a familiar route. Possibly my fate would have been similar to that of the bats that were being tested for a supposed sense of direction.

It is known that bats sometimes fly into tall buildings and flutter down with a broken neck, which suggests there are times when they shut off their echo-location. F. P. Möhres and T. Oettingen-Spielberg had a tame bat in a cage which they let out for exercise. After flying round for a while the bat would fly in through the door and suspend itself from its favourite roosting place. Several times the experimenters turned the cage through 90° or 180° while the bat was out. On its return the bat would try to fly in at the place where the door should have been, and it had then to search around for it. One day the experimenters removed the cage altogether while it was absent. On its return the bat flew in through the non-existent door and tried to suspend itself at its favourite roosting place, which had vanished.

When birds are nesting and the tree containing their nests is cut down they will sometimes spend days flying around where the tree used to stand and trying to land on a nest that is no longer there. The birds are presumably orientating themselves by the pattern of the landscape around. The tame bat was presumably orientating itself by the pattern of echoes in the room. But bats accustomed to flying through S-shaped tunnels will, when they are used to them, crash against a partition that is newly introduced to it. This can only mean that echo-location requires effort, and a bat flying through familiar surroundings probably switches off its echo-location.

Some years ago in London a social evening was organized once a week for blind people. The organizers had recruited a group of volunteers to bring the blind guests, none of whom lived very far away, to the meeting place and take them home again. One night, at the end of the evening, it was found that a thick fog had descended, with visibility nil. The blind guests took the helpers home.

To some extent, the birds that had lost their nest, the bats played tricks on by Möhres and Oettingen-Spielberg and certainly the blind guests, all relied on a spatial sense. The blind people were also using echo-location, not touch at a distance as has sometimes been suggested. This sense of distant touch, or being able to feel something without coming into contact with it, may exist among animals, and it has been postulated for moles especially, but there is no evidence for it with people. A woman who, years ago, claimed to be able while blindfolded to read print through her finger-tips attracted the attention of scientists until it was discovered she could peep under the bandage round her eyes. Exhaustive tests have set beyond reasonable doubt that blind people and blindfolded people can avoid walking into obstacles not because of distant touch but because they are hearing the faint echoes of their own footsteps and other sounds they themselves make and of which they may not be aware.

One result of researches inspired by the discovery of bats' use of sonar has been the discovery that many animals use an echo-location which is incidental. Rats, for example, have incisor teeth that grow continually at the roots. Consequently they must be as continually worn down. Without this they would grow 16 cm in a year. It used to be thought that rats kept their teeth in check by gnawing such things as wood, bones and concrete. A recent observation is that they are grinding their teeth, more or less all the time. These are the noises largely used in their echo-location. Tests on laboratory rats show that given two paths leading to food, one path being blocked by a vertical metal screen, a blindfolded rat will choose the other. If, however, the screen is at an angle of 45°, so that the echoes are deflected to one side, the rat will blunder into it. It will do so also if its ears are blocked.

An East African elephant shrew gives a further excellent example of the combined use of senses. It is called elephant shrew for its long, slender and mobile snout. Its hindlegs are markedly longer than its forelegs and its normal mode of progression is by leaps, recalling that of a kangaroo. When out foraging the elephant shrew follows well-defined runs in a far-reaching system of tracks that extend for hundreds of metres. Mainly these are along tunnels in the grass, but they often cross open ground over hard patches of soil where there are no tracks obvious to the human eye. Yet throughout the shrew always places its feet in the same places each time. At intervals the animal has boltholes under stones into which it will run to gain temporary respite from pursuit, emerging after an interval to continue on its way. And it seems always to know exactly where these are.

The shrew is active by day and by night, and if pursued closely will flee at high speed; yet it is always sure of where it is going, and it never fails to place its feet where it habitually puts them down. The whole of its behaviour suggests a clear and detailed memory of its

Still life picture of an East African elephant shrew *Elephantulus brachyrhynchus* bounding at high speed. Although only its feet touch the ground it always places these in the same places in its extensive runs, suggesting maximum combination of acute senses coupled with memory.

trails and of its environment generally, aided no doubt by its senses. Its eyes are large compared with those of true shrews, or even compared with rodents of the same size. The whiskers are long, the sense of smell is acute, and there is some evidence that the mobile snout may have a well-developed sense of touch.

How these senses are used can at present be only surmised. The elephant shrew, like all shrews, is continually active when not resting, moving about quickly. Its snout is continually on the move as well, and any insect in its path is investigated with the snout, by touch or by smell, or by the two together; it is impossible to be sure which is used. A large insect will be seized with the teeth. If the insect is small a very long tongue is shot out and the insect disappears at speed into the mouth so fast that the human eye cannot follow the movement. It is then pushed into a cheek pouch, to be consumed later, the elephant shrew extracting it and chewing even as it goes along.

From what can be seen, the elephant shrew is doing everything at high speed yet with remarkable precision, which would be impossible without a highly efficient co-ordination of all the senses.

Chapter 15

The unseen senses

It is fitting that we should end this account of animal senses with the pineal eye, the organ with which we started the book. There is probably no other animal structure that has been so closely and repeatedly studied and about which scientists have speculated more than this third eye, which we now find is the remains of a second pair of eyes.

In the brain of every living mammal, lying in the centre of its upper surface and hidden by the cerebral hemispheres, is a small white structure shaped like a pine cone. It was first discovered in the human brain by Greek anatomists over two thousand years ago, although it is only 6 mm long and weighs only 0·1 gm. Galen, a Greek physician in the second century A.D., who continued the study of this organ, noted that it was unpaired and lying in a central position, and suggested it was a kind of valve regulating the flow of thought from the main part of the brain.

In the seventeenth century René Descartes, the brilliant French philosopher, took this idea further. He is usually quoted, with somewhat derisory overtones, as having identified the pineal body as the seat of the soul, because alone among the sense-organs it is unpaired. In fact he suggested it was the seat of the rational soul, that our eyes looking out into the world transmit what they see to the pineal, which allows fluids to flow through hollow tubes to the muscles, prompting them to take appropriate action. In the light of what is now known about the pineal in mammals, this was not so wide of the truth as it has been made out to be.

There the matter rested until 1910, when Arthur Dendy published his classical description of the pineal eye of the tuatara, the New Zealand lizard, and the brain structures associated with it. He found, by cutting thin slices of the brain of tuatara and examining these under a microscope, that beneath a small opening in the top of the skull was a tiny eye, 0·5 mm diameter, with a retina and a lens, and with a slender nerve running to the brain. Also rising from the top of the brain was a second structure, the parapineal, which seemed to be the even more degenerate remains of a second eye. A pineal eye or its equivalent, such as the 'pine cone' on the mammalian brain, can be found in all but a few vertebrates. Moreover there is a hole in the top of the skull of many fossil reptiles above where the pineal eye would have been in life. It seemed natural to conclude that the earliest vertebrates had a pair of eyes in the top of the head, either in addition to the eyes at the side, or else before the lateral eyes were evolved.

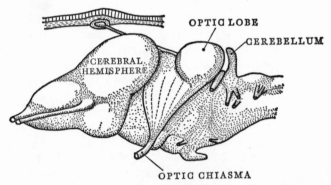

Brain of a reptile in side view showing the pineal eye on its slender stalk lying just beneath the skin covering the top of the skull. The pineal eye, remains of a pair of eyes on the top of the head, is found in various stages of degeneration in reptiles.

In 1898 Otto Heubner, a physician, treated a boy who had a pineal tumour and also suffered from precocious puberty. During the next fifty years other similar cases were studied, but all that could be concluded was that the pineal might have something to do with the control of the sexual organs. Meanwhile anatomists had been finding a pineal eye or its equivalent in one species of vertebrate after another, in fishes, amphibians, reptiles, birds and mammals. It was better developed in some animals, that is, looking more like an eye; more degenerate in some and looking more like a gland in others. It is not present in the brains of snakes, which are believed to have descended from ancestors that lived underground, and it is also absent from some other subterranean reptiles. On the other hand, reptiles known as blind-worms, because they have no eyes at the sides of the head, can tell night from day because they have this third eye.

Lampreys have two eye-like structures on the top of the brain, and these are used in detecting light. The nearest living relative of lampreys, the hagfish, has no trace of them. The hagfish is, however, degenerate in many other ways and it also shuns the light. In 1918 N. Holmgren examined the pineal of a dogfish and a frog. In both of these he found sensory cells which bore a marked resemblance to the cone cells of a normal retina. Moreover there were nerve cells associated with them, suggesting that in these two animals the pineal was in some way a light-sensitive organ. Forty years later E. Dodt showed that the pineal of a frog converts light of certain wavelengths into nervous impulses, although what part this plays in the life of the frog is still uncertain. In 1963 Ingrid de la Motte carried out experiments on trout and pike. She blindfolded them by putting covers over their ordinary eyes and placed them in a tank in complete darkness. She flashed a lamp and put food in the corner of the tank. In a short while she had trained the fishes by the usual conditioning methods to look for food whenever she flashed the lamp. This showed, first of all, that the fishes could detect light with their third eye. What is more remarkable is that the light in the signalling lamp was dimmed more and more until the human eye could hardly see it, yet the fishes still reacted immediately to it.

Researches on lizards have shown that there are differences in the pineal from one species to another, if only in small details. In the footless lizard of California the hole in the skull has almost closed and the eye beneath it is smaller than usual. This lizard spends nearly all its time burrowing in sandhills. Its relative, the slow-worm of Europe, has a larger opening in the skull and a larger pineal eye, and although the slow-worm spends much of its time underground it often comes onto the surface and, even when underground, frequently rests with its head exposed. In some species of lizard the differences are more obvious in regard to the nerve connecting the eye to the brain. It may be fairly well developed, with as many as 250 nerve fibres, or it may be so feeble that it is impossible to trace a connection with the brain.

In many lizards this third eye tells them when to change colour because the colour of the light which reaches the pineal gland through this eye makes it produce more or fewer hormones, and these in turn cause a change in the reptile's skin. After a very few minutes a lizard's colour resembles that of the light reaching it, producing an ideal camouflage. In some lizards the third eye controls the length of time they bask in the sun. Although reptiles are cold-blooded, and do not become active until they have warmed up, they very rapidly suffer from heat stroke. It seems that the third eye tells them when they have had enough, but it probably tells them this in an odd way. Thus experiments on the third eye of other animals suggest that it sometimes acts as an organ to stop an animal doing something. It is an inhibitor. It seems possible that this is what is happening with a basking lizard, and that the lizard is lying still because its third eye is telling it to, by inhibiting movement of its legs, and when this third eye warms up to a degree approaching danger point it goes out of action—the inhibitor is no longer working, and the lizard gets up and walks away.

Most of the researches on this enigmatic organ in the brain of vertebrates have been somewhat inconclusive, and the results have been so varied that they can be summarized only in general terms. We can say that the pineal eye and its associated structures seem to represent a pair of eyes which, in the early vertebrates, may have been fully functional eyes. If that is so, then we can pass to the next generalization, that in living vertebrates the second pair of eyes has either disappeared altogether, as in the hagfish and in snakes, or has changed its function. The third positive statement we can make is that the change in function varies from one group of vertebrates to another. In all, however, they seem to involve the perception of light, and in some there seems to be a connection between the pineal and the sexual organs.

During the last twelve years researches on the pineal body have been taken a step further, although still without reaching a firm conclusion. They are nevertheless of unusual interest. It seems certain, for example, that in mammals the pineal body is a gland that produces two hormones. One of these is called serotonin and is produced in response to light. The other, melatonin, is produced in conditions of darkness. One reason for saying this is that rats produce more serotonin when kept permanently illuminated, and less when kept constantly in the dark.

The other conclusion that emerges from these researches is that when light stimulates the retina of the ordinary eye information is transmitted to the pineal through the sympathetic nerves. This works a biological clock in the pineal. Other information is transmitted from the brain, but is also dependent on light from the outside world, and this works a second biological clock.

Melatonin seems to influence the breeding cycles in the female mammal. Serotonin tends to inhibit them. The amount of light and darkness, at least in temperate regions, varies with the seasons and so alters the balance between melatonin and serotonin. This may trigger the ripening of the reproductive organs, thus determining the breeding cycles of birds and of mammals that breed once yearly. Melatonin also synchronizes some daily rhythms.

It is hardly possible to say more without becoming involved in lengthy biochemical details, but it looks as if the pineal could control the circadian rhythm and the monthly and yearly cycles by its two biological clocks. In saying this one is guessing, or, more precisely, trying to express in a few words the impressions one gets from reading what those who have investigated the pineal organs have written. It may well be proved in the future that the pineal body in the human brain comes very near to being what Descartes thought it was: the seat of the rational soul which, stimulated by the light reaching the eye, sends fluids to the muscles and so governs the working of the body. If for 'fluids' we read 'hormones' and substitute 'seat of control' for 'rational soul' Descartes seems to have been not far out in his guess. All we need then is to find out what it is that the hormones stimulate, so governing the workings of the body. To a large extent it is the proprioceptors, or proprioceptive system. So far no definite link has been established between the pineal and the proprioceptors, but there is still a long way to go in the study of both of these.

Compared with the compact, well-defined and specialized sense-organs such as the eye, ear and nose, the proprioceptive system of sense-organs is diffuse and has therefore been largely neglected. The system registers less obvious stimuli than do the specialized senses, and has usually been held responsible for what is called the kinaesthetic sense, or muscle sense, which registers the deformations and stresses in the body arising from an animal's own movements. That is, the proprioceptors tell us how we move our muscles, and they are located especially in the muscles and tendons and in the joints, the proprioceptors of the joints being in the membranes covering the bone.

The proprioceptors are therefore internal sense-organs, whereas all the others are at the surface, except for the semicircular canals in the ear, which are sometimes included with the proprioceptive senses, and the temperature receptors. It is through them that an animal establishes the relationship of each part of the body to the rest and the relationship of the body as a whole to the outside world. They are served by nerves running to the muscles, and if these could be brought together into two main nerves they would, as H. W. Lissmann has said, be of such impressive proportions that no student of biology could ignore them. As it is, the proprioceptors are small, are never seen, and we are so used to them from the moment we are born that we are unaware of them. Indeed in 1949 G. H. Bourne wrote: 'Man is said to have five senses, although really he has six, the sixth being the proprioceptive sense, the sense of muscular position.'

Because our knowledge of these senses lags behind that of the other senses it is not proposed to do more here than mention their existence. It will do no harm, however, first to correct what must surely be a wrong impression given by many who have written about the proprioceptors. They suggest, for example, that every time we put food into our mouths, although no one has ever seen his own mouth except in a mirror, we are relying on our proprioceptive senses to know exactly where the mouth is. This must surely be not the whole truth. Finding our mouths can only be done because very early in infancy we have learned by trial and error where the mouth is. One has only to watch a baby in its early efforts at feeding itself to realize this. Later, memory and the proprioceptors work together. Similarly, they say, whenever we put a hand in a pocket to take something out the hand goes exactly to where the pocket is. Again, we can only do this on the basis of past experience, and again it is the proprioceptive senses working in conjunction with memory.

A quadruped, these same writers tell us, puts its hindfeet to the ground without seeing them move—probably does not need to watch its forefeet either—and in jumping an obstacle it looks at this before jumping, but its proprioceptive senses carry the hindfeet over without the aid of the eyes. So far as a quadruped jumping an obstacle is concerned, anyone who has watched young animals at all closely will know that the first attempts to jump are a failure. The young quadruped has to learn to jump by trial and error, using vision and touch, and only later do the proprioceptive senses take over the task of guiding it. A puppy first exploring its environment will try to jump over a low obstacle in its path. It will make a most determined spring and as likely as not end up on its belly, spreadeagled across the obstacle. Very soon, however, it will have learned to jump with confidence, and we can only assume there has to be some form of education of the central nervous system, based on trial and error, and linked with the memory of past experiences.

On a dark night we put our feet to the ground, and although touch helps in this it is not essential, as in cold weather, for example, when we lose all feeling in our feet. We can still walk. The nerve-endings in the muscle cells are still stimulated by the movements of the muscles. Nerve-endings in the tendons are still responding when the tendons are stretched. And others in the membranes covering the joints are still stimulated by the contacts between the surfaces of the joints. Presumably we could not do this had we not first learned to walk in daylight—but how far, in taking our first steps in early infancy, we watch our feet or the ground would be hard to say.

Nevertheless these examples of walking in the dark or with numbed feet illustrate well the important part played in our lives by the proprioceptors.

There are other instances in which, perhaps, too much has been attributed to the proprioceptors. Thus it is assumed by some investigators that a nocturnal animal finds its way about in the dark using its kinaesthetic sense, or, in other words, its proprioceptive system. This is true, but with the same qualification as we have been discussing. It is difficult to see how an animal can use this system alone any more effectively than one that is moving about in daylight except by linking it with a memory of its surroundings, and also by making greater use of senses other than vision. One writer, for example, expresses wonder at the way a man will put his hand out in the dark and place it accurately on a banister rail, implying that he uses his kinaesthetic sense to do this. The fact is, however, that he could not do so were he not also familiar with the position of the rail, just as my genet (see Chapter 14) made itself familiar with its new surroundings.

There are, however, other ways in which these internal senses help us which seem not to depend on memory or learning of any kind. Proprioceptive nerve-endings tell us when the stomach is empty, by the over-contraction of the muscles in the wall of the intestine. They also tell us when to stretch and when to yawn. Thus when we rest the blood tends to circulate sluggishly in the veins. After a while we stretch and the action of the muscles squeezes the veins, sending the blood more quickly to the heart to be purified. When we yawn we fill the lungs deeply and send the blood in their walls on its way to the heart to send the oxygen it contains more quickly to the rest of the body. And it is our proprioceptors that inform us when we are feeling refreshed.

So far as yawning is concerned we probably need to differentiate between yawning when we are tired and yawning after waking first thing in the morning. In the former, the yawn is probably in response to the need for more oxygen in the blood to offset muscle fatigue. In the latter, it is in response to the need to get the circulation moving again. The principle is the same in the two cases but the effects are different.

In the present inadequate state of our knowledge of the workings of the pineal and of the proprioceptors we can only guess at some of the other effects they may have, separately or in combination. Perhaps they hold the key to at least one question everyone of adult years must have pondered: why a touch of sunlight can so quickly raise our spirits, quicken our steps, banish despondency and make life seem altogether different from what it was previously.

It seems also to be true of animals. The nightingale, for example, has a high reputation as a song-bird, and its name reflects its habit of singing by night. But nightingales sing by day also, although their voices are then lost in the general chorus of spring song. Although so much has been written about the nightingale's night singing there is nothing to compare with the superlative music the same bird will pour out on a sunny morning in spring. Until it is proved otherwise, there must remain the suspicion that either the pineal or the proprio-ceptors, or the two in combination, revitalize the metabolism of the nightingale on such occasions, making it sing its heart out. And it is on just such a morning that we also feel so uplifted, even by merely seeing the sunshine through the window, without any of it coming into the room.

So much of what is said in this chapter is speculative, and certainly it is still impossible to trace a direct link between the pineal and the 'workings of the body' (the proprioceptors). There is, however, just the suspicion that a future von Frisch, Griffin or Matthews may suddenly make a breakthrough, as these investigators did with the breathtaking stories of celestial navigation and echo-location. Then the floodgates will open for new and unsuspected knowledge on the internal senses that have for so long been ignored—with sunlight, through the pineal, via the eyes meaning more to us than we now suspect.

Index

Index

Index

plover, Egyptian, 87
porpoise, 62
prawn, 18, 21, 22, 26, 27, 45, 77
proprioceptor, 174–7
Pumphrey, R. J., 64

rabbit, 49, 86, 94, 115, 122, 123
rat, 10, 11, 64, 94, 118, 168, 173
rat, kangaroo, 53, 54
Rathmayer, W., 14
rattlesnake, 54, 89, 90
ray, 5, 67, 72, 73, 75, 76
receptor cell, 2, 3, 5
red mullet, 101
reptile, 46, 47, 87, 110, 120, 138, 171
rhinoceros, 118
Rhodnius, 79
rhodopsin, 106
ringlet butterfly, 82
robber bee, 39
rockling, 101
rodents, 16, 53, 119, 154, 165, 169
Roeder, Kenneth D., 52, 53, 98, 99
Romanes, G. J., 108
rook, 102, 103
Ross, Mr, 146
round window, 42

sacculus, 19, 20, 21, 22, 42, 45
sagitta, 22
salamander, 46
salmon, 35, 112, 143
sandhopper, 135, 141, 144, 154
Sauer, E. G. F., 133, 136, 137, 138–9, 140,
    141, 144, 150
sawfly, 136, 161
scallop, 128
Schmidt, Bastian, 110, 137
scorpion, 22
sea-anemone, 11, 12, 13, 40, 96, 107, 146,
    147, 148
sea lion, 66
sea urchin, 127, 146
seal, 17, 65
semicircular canal, 42
serotonin, 173
shanny, 146
shark, 5, 72, 111–12
shearwater, 139, 162
sheep, 121
shrew, 64, 147, 168, 169
shrimp, 26, 45
silk moth, 105
silverfish, 117
skate, 5, 73, 75
slow-worm, 172
Smallman, R. L., 94
snakes, 19, 31, 46, 47, 54, 89, 90, 91, 101,
    171, 173
snapping turtle, 110
sonar, 6, 56, 58, 63, 65, 168
Spallanzani, Lazaro, 57

spiders, 9, 14, 22, 23, 36–8, 130
sponge, 9
squid, 128
squirrels, 32, 33, 82, 115, 119, 121
stag beetle, 51
stapes, 41, 44, 58, 59
stargazer, 76
starlings, 137, 154
statocyst, 21, 22, 27
statolith, 21
stirrup, 46
sturgeon, 100
sunfish, 45
swallow, 124, 125
swan, 124
swift, 124, 125, 162
swiftlet, 64, 155

tapetum, 127
taste-bud, 101
temperature receptor, 5
termitaria, 79
termite, 79
tern, 126
Thornton, W. M., 76, 77
toad, 46, 101, 138, 143, 144
tolylurea, 95
Treat, A. E., 53
trilobites, 25
Triops, 25, 26
trout, 172
tuatara, ix, 170
turtle, 110, 143, 159–61
tympanic bulla, 53, 54
tympanic membrane, 53
Tyschenko, V. P., 155
Tyto alba, 48

Uca, 149
ultrasonics, 3, 44, 52, 58, 61–5, 72
upside-down fish, 28
utriculus, 19, 20, 22, 42, 45

vibrissae, 14
vole, 64
von Frisch, Karl, ix, 1, 4, 130–7, 141, 177

walrus, 17
warbler, 139, 140, 141, 144, 150
wasp, 97, 98, 116, 130, 131
water beetle, 100
water bug, 28
water-flea, 40, 141
Waterman, Talbot H., 141, 142
weakfish, 45
Wenzel, Bernice, 110
whale, 62, 109
whirligig beetle, 25, 126
wild boar, 115
wolf, 115
woodlouse, 18
wrasses, 27